New method in social science

Jon-Arild Johannessen

ISBN-13:978-1535423823

ISBN-10:153542382X

CONTENTS

ACKNOWLEDGMENTS

We would like to express our thanks to Assistant Professor Siri Hopland, Kristiania University College, Norway, for making the book more reader-friendly than we could have managed ourselves. We would also like to thank Live Vikøren, the Senior Librarian at Kristiania University College, for all the assistance she provided.

Part I: Theory

Chapter 1: Conceptual generalisation

• Introduction

Research falls into two main categories: conceptual generalisation and empirical generalisation.[1] Conceptual generalisation is an investigation whereby the researcher uses other researchers' empirical findings in conjunction with his or her own process of conceptualisation in order to generalise and identify a pattern. This contrasts with empirical generalisation, where the researcher investigates a phenomenon or problem that is apparent in the empirical data, and only thereafter generalises in the light of his or her own findings.[2] The starting point for the researcher in the case of both empirical and conceptual generalisation will be a phenomenon or problem in the social world.

We will now investigate the following question: How can we use conceptual generalisation in social science? This problem gives rise to two research questions:

---

[1] Bunge, 1998:3-50, 51-107, 403-411 (Volume One). In particular, see Bunge, 1998:17.
[2] Bunge, 1988:403-411 (Volume One).

1. What are conceptual models?

2. How can we develop conceptual models?

If we can solve this problem, we will also have made a small contribution to methodology in social science.

Conceptual generalisation and empirical generalisation are strategies that are available for answering scientific questions. Which of these strategies one chooses to use will be determined largely by the nature of the problem and "the subject matter, and on the state of our knowledge regarding that subject matter."[3] Conceptual generalisation, which is the subject of our investigation here, is "a procedure applying to the whole cycle of investigation into every problem of knowledge."[4]

This book is based on a theoretical and philosophical scientific perspective known as the systemic approach. This approach was developed by Mario Bunge[5] and systematised by Johannessen & Olaisen.[6] We will not examine the systemic approach in any further detail in this book.

---

[3] Bunge, 1998:16.
[4] Bunge, 1998:9.
[5] See references to Mario Bunge in the bibliography.
[6] Johannessen & Olaisen, 2005; 2006; 2006a.

The book is structured as follows. Part I is devoted to answering Research Question 1: What are conceptual models? Part II is devoted to answering Research Question 2: How can we develop conceptual models? Finally, there are three conclusions. In Conclusion I, we apply the outcomes of Parts I and II in order to answer the problem set forth at the beginning of this book. In Conclusion II, we examine some of the practical implications of our investigation. In Conclusion III, we reflect on some of the theoretical implications of our investigation.

Fig. 1 shows a conceptual model that summarises the introduction and indicates how this book is structured.

Figure 1. How can we use conceptual generalisation in social science?

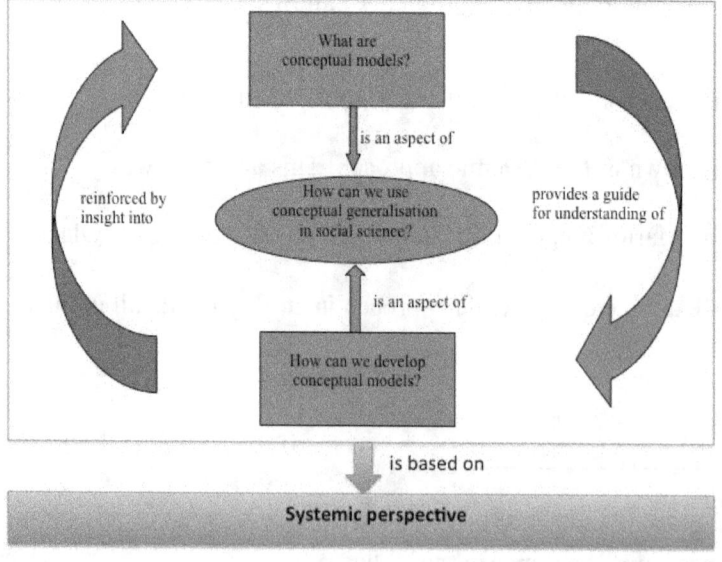

• What are conceptual models?

Concepts and conceptual models are described and discussed in great depth by Deleuze & Guattari.[7] In their book *What is Philosophy?*, Deleuze & Guattari give a verbal definition of a conceptual model as one which develops concepts and shows the relations between them, together with the application of the concepts.[8]

The philosopher Mario Bunge has also discussed conceptual models and conceptual generalisation in several of his books.[9] The sociologist Jonathan Turner is recognized as the person who has conducted perhaps the most in-depth examination of conceptual models and conceptual generalisation in social science.[10]

A conceptual model can be applied in order to generate innovative ideas, which may have theoretical and/or practical relevance. This type of model consists – as the term suggests – of concepts. These concepts are made up of components. In the same way that indicators must be developed when measuring the results from practical experiments, we

---

[7] Deleuze & Guattari, 2011.
[8] Deleuze & Guattari, 2011:15-35.
[9] Bunge, 1983; 1983a; 1985; 1985a; 1996; 1997; 1997a; 1998; 1998b; 1998c; 2001a; 2003; 2009; 2014.
[10] Turner, 1987; 1988; 2002; 2007; 2013.

need components and their essential properties in order to say something about the concept inherent to a conceptual model.

Conceptual models are always related to a problem or a phenomenon; without this relation, they would cease to have meaning or purpose. However, it must be noted that they only capture an aspect of the phenomenon or problem (a particular aspect or perspective of reality[11]) that they are attempting to represent, or as expressed by Deleuze & Guattari: "…as it appears to me."[12]

What is a concept? When we see or imagine something in the outside world, we say that we form "percepts of it"[13]. "Percepts" attempt to capture objects that are perceived or imagined[14]. Concepts, however, bear no similar resemblance to what they represent; they are constructed abstractions, not physical representations. We may say there are two types of concepts[15]:

1. Those which originate from a process of perception, and

2. Those which do not originate from a process of perception.

We may call them **empirical**, and **transempirical**, respectively[16]. An

---

[11] Asplund, 1970; 2010.
[12] Deleuze & Guattari, 2011:16.
[13] Bunge, 1983:159 (Volume 5).
[14] Bunge, 1983:159 (Volume 5).
[15] Bunge, 1983:159-163 (Volume 5).

empirical concept may be understood as being analogous to a map, whereas a transempirical concept may be understood as being analogous to the symbols used on the map.

Examples of transempirical concepts are function, field, continuity and infinity. Metaphorically, a transempirical concept may be said to be like a car registration plate. A car registration plate says very little generally about a car, but an expert will nevertheless be able to ascertain much information about the car from its plate. According to Albert Einstein, most concepts in quantum physics are transempirical[17] and in this connection he says, "there is no inductive method which could lead to the fundamental concepts of physics"[18].

Concepts have a history and stand in relation to other concepts that constitute the conceptual model we develop to focus on a particular

---

[16] From an epistemological standpoint, there are differing views here. Idealists deny the existence of empirical concepts, or say they are dependent on trans-empirical concepts, whereas empiricists deny the existence of trans-empirical concepts (cf. Bunge, 1983: 159-174). From a "realism" or systemic perspective, some concepts may be said to have their origins in "percepts", while others do not.

In the following, due to space limitation and pedagogical considerations, we will not consider the various discussions in the philosophy of science concerning these points. We would, though, like to bring to the reader's attention the important role the philosophy of science and scientific theory play in the formulation of different perspectives, including the development of concepts, conceptual models and conceptual generalisations.

[17] Einstein, 1936:353.

[18] Einstein, 1936:365.

problem or phenomenon[19]. Conceptual models, like most other models, are fragmentary in the sense that they do not depict physical reality like a photograph; they only show a certain perspective of reality. The analogy we might use here could be a house that is observed by two scientists making observations on either side of the house, and two other scientists also making observation inside the house looking out the windows on either side. The scientists standing outside the house are talking on the phone and comparing observations; obviously their observations differ, as they have different perspectives. Similarly, the scientists inside the house looking out into the outside world also report differing views of what they observe. The differing views may not be relative, but they are all real and objective; however, they only reveal aspects of "reality", from the point of view (perspective) of the individual researcher. This analogy attempts to show that when a researcher observes a problem/phenomenon in the social world, then he/she does this on the basis of three main processes[20]:

---

[19] Deleuze & Guattari, 2011:18-22.
[20] Bateson, 1988:60; Maturana & Varela, 1992; Bandler & Grinder, 1982; 1990.

1. We select something from a phenomenon or problem area; we also choose to discard much of what is contained in the field of the phenomenon/problem area.

2. What we choose to discard is generalised through abstraction processes.

3. In these abstraction processes, that which we have selected is altered and distorted in relation to its origin. This is no more complex than the fact that data differs from information, which again differs from knowledge.

The concepts in a conceptual model are not so much variables, but: "—in the concept there are only ordinate relationships [...] pure and simple variations ordered according to their neighbourhood."[21] A conceptual model emerges in relation to its composition, relationships between concepts and the phenomenon or problem model it refers to, as shown in Figure 2.

---

[21] Deleuze & Guattari, 2011:20.

Figure 2. Schematic representation of a conceptual model.

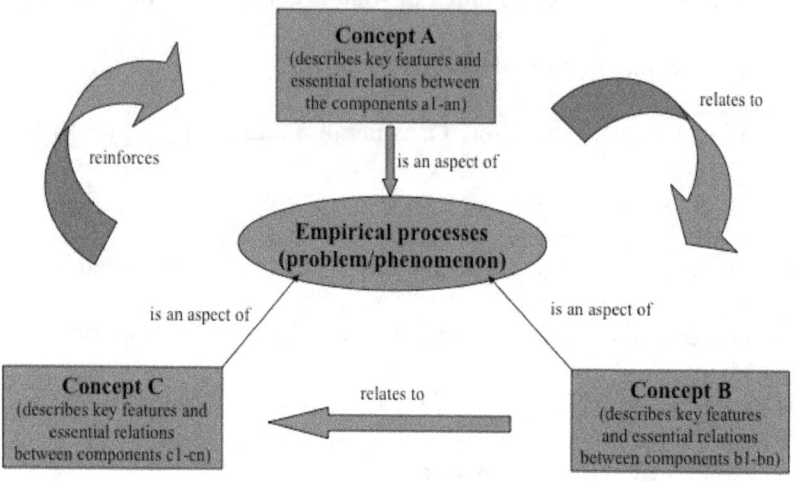

In the natural sciences and mathematics, models are formalized and are relatively unambiguous[22]. In the social sciences models may be developed in different ways, from formal mathematical relationships to more loose analytical frameworks, interactive (circular) analytical models, linear causal models and empirical causal models. This study will restrict itself to the use of the term conceptual model as showing concepts and their relations as a visual figure "that maps properties of the social universe and their interrelations."[23] A conceptual model based on this understanding is thus a diagrammatic representation of various relations. The concepts are designed so that they denote a system[24] of

---

[22] Turner, 1987:164.
[23] Turner, 1987:164.

components that constitute central key features of the concept. The components have such relationships to each other and give meaning to the concept precisely because of their key features and their relationships.

Based on this understanding, a conceptual model is a representation of aspects, activities, processes, etc., which reveal an action or event in practice. The above sentence may be understood as *a process definition of a conceptual model*. The conceptual model uses concepts and components to highlight relations in the phenomenon or problem being studied. The visual conceptual model shows how concepts are related to each other and also how the components are related to the concept. In addition, the conceptual model shows how it is related to the phenomenon/problem being studied.

The purpose of conceptual models is to model a problem or phenomenon such that its generic properties are isolated. Further, the purpose is to understand or explain the nature of the phenomenon/problem. Conceptual models can be designed at different levels of abstraction, and relate to the few or many empirical studies that the conceptual model is based on.

---

[24] System: components that have relationships with each other and a boundary to the outside world.

• How can we develop conceptual models?

Part II is structured as follows: First, *different conceptual models* will be examined. Second, a schematic *typology of the different conceptual models* is presented. Finally, *a strategy for the development of conceptual models* will be discussed.

The various conceptual models

The following four main types of <u>conceptual models</u> are presented in the following. These are:

1. Thought experiments

2. Analytical schemes: These consist of analytical frameworks and analytical models

3. Empirical causal models and case studies

4. "Data mining" models

Thought experiments

A thought experiment has a very high level of abstraction, but few, if any, empirical studies that support it. It is to a large extent modelled on perception, and characterised by the use of analogy and figurative language.

In Greek philosophy, the thought experiment (*deiknymi*) was used to highlight conceptual correlations. In the history of philosophy, Plato's Cave Allegory is perhaps the most well-known thought experiment. In the history of science, the oldest thought experiment is perhaps Galileo's observations concerning the velocity of falling objects in a vacuum. On the basis of this thought experiment, Galileo rejected Aristotle's law of gravity. Whether or not Galileo transformed his thought experiment to a practical experiment in the leaning tower of Pisa is still a topic for discussion among historians of science. In the context of this study, thought experiments are of great interest because they may have major implications for both theory and practice.

In the scientific field, thought experiments have been used by, among others, Einstein, Podolsky and Rosen. In what is referred to as the EPR paradox, the three scientists attempted to show that Heisenberg's uncertainty principle did not provide an adequate explanation in quantum physics. Another famous thought experiment is Schrødinger's cat.

The importance of the thought experiment for scientific methodology was particularly emphasised by the philosopher and science theorist Paul Feyerabend[25], and also by the philosopher and science theorist Mario Bunge[26]. An important purpose of thought experiments is to apply them as hypothetical scenarios in order to highlight a few key points, and to examine the possible consequences of a research question.

A thought experiment may be defined as an experiment in which controlled mental actions are performed by a person in relation to a phenomenon or problem area with the purpose of solving a theoretical or practical problem[27]. However, a thought experiment is not considered to be a so-called genuine experiment, but consists of imagining what would happen if certain facts were to occur or if they had not occurred[28]. Bunge says of thought experiments (German: *Gedankeneexperimente*) that they, "have no validating force, but they may spark off interesting hypotheses." [29]

A thought experiment may be understood on the basis of the three cognitive processes: Attribution, association and generalisation[30].

---

[25] Feyerabend, 1993.
[26] Bunge, 1999; 2000; 2001.
[27] Bunge, 1997a:126.
[28] Bunge, 1997a:126.
[29] Bunge, 1997a:126.
[30] Bunge, 1983:174.

Attribution is when we attribute a property or a relationship to an object, phenomenon or problem. For instance, we may see an apple fall from a tree and attribute this to the property of the force of gravity (Newton's thought experiment). Thus, in the process of attribution we see or perceive something, and then conjecture an attributing property; thus we move from sensory perception to the development of concepts through a generalisation process. In other words, we move from the empirical level (sensory perception) to a level of abstraction (the concepts) which is not directly linked to the empirical level. This occurs by making conjectures regarding possible relations until at some point we are satisfied (without being certain) that our assumptions are correct. In other words, we shape conceptual relations, and on the basis of this attribution process we develop a thought experiment. In the example mentioned above of the falling apple, Newton is believed to have "discovered" the law of gravity. Thought experiments are often tested out empirically to substantiate the accuracy of the presumed relations; thus, one of the results of a thought experiment might be a testable hypothesis.

In *association,* different domains are related to each other in order to create something new. For instance, Stafford Beer's viable system model (VSM) draws similarities between management and organisation and the structure and function of the human brain[31]. Association can be carried out in different ways. Associations may be made to natural phenomena; a beehive has a very special form of organisation, and a few "simple rules" that ensure high productivity in the collection of nectar, often called "the dance of the bees"[32]. It is easy to imagine how this natural phenomenon could be associated with ideas concerning the design and operation of an effective public or private organisation (especially how teamwork can be facilitated). Associations may take place at various levels and between different types of objects and social systems. However, it is always the phenomenon or the problem area that is the starting point of an association. Other examples of association within the natural world could involve an examination of how bird flocks, schools of fish, swarms of bees, colonies of ants and so on, work together in order to survive. On the basis of such an association, it would be possible to develop the concept of "flocking" which further could be applied to the design of conceptual models where "flocking" was the phenomenon under investigation (for instance, in human organisations). Another example could concern an examination of Schumpeter's concept of creative destruction. In this context, it may be of interest to examine what happens in the years after a forest fire. In this example, destruction is a prerequisite for the growth of new trees (the "creative new" in

---

[31] Beer, 1979; 1985.
[32] Facklam & Johnson, 1992.

Schumpeter's concept). Associations need not be "true". The point is that they initiate ideas that can be used in a thought experiment.

There are two types of *generalisation*. The first type is based on similar cases which are compared over time and where we attempt to find a pattern, often referred to as a type of inductive generalisation. Pavlov's classic conditioning experiment with dogs provides such an example. Dogs were exposed to the sound of a tone shortly before feeding, and after a period of time they would salivate in response to the tone before receiving food.

The second type is based on individual cases, where we look for a transfer of learning or experience; for instance, how a specific organisation was able to develop an innovative information and learning system that resulted an increase in both innovation and productivity. A process of generalisation would involve a transfer of experience to other organisations, i.e. they would adopt the same system used in the specific case.

An important purpose of generalisation is that we condense information so that we can, for example, quickly infer an effective response from a signal. Generalisation helps us to economise our resources; however, it may also lead to inaccuracy.

While experiments might be said to be more important than observations[33], we can also say that thought experiments are a necessary precondition for real-world experiments. On the basis of such an understanding, it is appropriate to place the thought experiment in the top left corner of the schematic typology in Fig. 4.

When developing a thought experiment, we seek to build a bridge between that which is observable and that which is not. While a carpenter measures a length of wood using his/her ruler, a researcher measures by means of indicators, symptoms (e.g. the temperature of a patient), and markers (that which is observable). However, it is that which is not observable that we really are interested in, such as the disease behind a high fever or the tacit knowledge that is possessed by an expert but not by a novice. This understanding concerning indicators is important because in many cases we cannot come directly to grips with a phenomenon or problem. You often have to begin with indicators and key features of the components in a conceptual model (for instance, in a thought experiment).

Fig 3 Thought experiment

---

[33] Bunge, 2014:121.

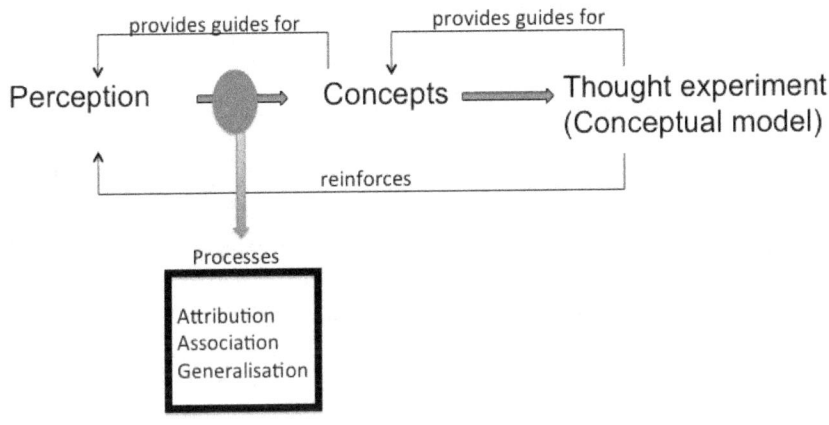

- Analytical scheme: Analytical frameworks and analytical models

We use here the collective term analytical scheme for the two types of conceptual models: analytical frameworks and analytical models.

The difference between a framework and a model is simple. A framework is defined as a system of concepts or components, with relationships between them, but with no direction regarding the relationships. A model is similar to a framework, but in addition there is direction regarding the relationships; for example, words such as 'influence', 'reinforce', 'inhibit', 'promote', etc., are used to describe these relationships (cf. Fig. 2). Analytical schemes also include other types of figurative and non-figurative representations of relationships or arrangements of information for a purpose, such as tables of various kinds, Gantt charts, and so on.

An analytical model has a higher level of abstraction than an analytical framework, and is based on empirical studies to a greater degree[34] (cf. Fig. 4). It is also more specific than an analytical framework, because it provides a deeper understanding of the relationships between concepts and components, cf. the formal definition of a conceptual model in Part I.

An analytical scheme consists of a construction of abstract systems, where key concepts in a conceptual generalisation and the relationship between them emerges. Its purpose is to come to grips with the dynamic processes in the phenomenon/problem being investigated. It is like attempting to gain insight into a bird's flight characteristics while it is flying rather than by dissecting it.

In an analytical scheme, we try to explain how specific events affect the phenomenon in focus: for example, how innovation (event I) affects economic crises (event II). Both event I and event II relate to specific empirical processes. An analytical scheme, say Giddens & Turner, may also be used to "construct a descriptive scenario."[35]

There are thus two ways in which analytical schemes may be used: first,

---

[34] Turner, 1987:159-195.
[35] Giddens & Turner, 1987:162.

to explain relationships between event I and event II, and second, to apply such analytical schemes in an attempt to construct certain scenarios given certain conditions. In this context, Giddens & Turner speak of "naturalistic analytical schemes and sensitizing analytical schemes"[36].

An analytical scheme is an overarching analysis tool, which can be used to illuminate and organise a phenomenon, event, action or process[37]. The purpose of an analytical scheme is: "...the construction of abstract systems of categories that presumably denote key properties of the universe and crucial relations among those properties. [...] Explanation of specific events is achieved when the scheme can be used to interpret some specific empirical process."[38] Methodologically, an analytical scheme may be used in two ways, according to Turner. First, when you match an empirical event with the concepts of the scheme, "then the empirical event is considered to be explained."[39] Second, "when the scheme can be used to construct a descriptive scenario, of why and how events in an empirical situation transpired, then these events are seen as explained."[40]

---

[36] Giddens & Turner, 1987:162.
[37] Turner, 1987:162.
[38] Turner, 1987:162.
[39] Turnes, 1987:162.
[40] Turner, 1987:162.

For some, especially those who use "naturalistic analytical schemes", the analytical scheme is sufficient to establish relationships and find patterns in a social system. For others, especially those who use "sensitizing analytical schemes", the analytical scheme is a necessary but not a sufficient condition for uncovering such patterns. Researchers who use "sensitizing analytical schemes" believe that the sufficient condition is to be found when using insights from analytical schemes to examine empirical relationships in their own data, and then construct empirical causal models to visualise these relationships[41].

• Empirical causal models and case studies

Empirical causals models will be discussed first, and then case studies.

Empirical causal models

Empirical causal models may be developed in two ways. The first approach is related to hypothetical deductive thinking, where the model is developed on the basis of an established theory. A theory is defined here as a "system of propositions"[42]. A proposition is defined here as two

---

[41] Bunge, 1999; Turner, 1987:156-195.
[42] Bunge, 1983:331, cf. also 331-345 for an explanation of the theory

or more variables connected to statements of the type: the more of one, the greater the likelihood that the other variable decreases or increases[43].

When these propositions are rewritten as operational hypotheses and tested against empirical data, then new empirical causal models can be developed. These models then show quantitative relations between variables in the original empirical causal model. The quantitative model is a visualisation of the relationships in the empirical data.

The second approach for developing empirical causal models occurs when there exists an established theory in the field. One method involves using "Grounded Theory"[44], or other inductive methods.

Fig. 4 Empirical causal models

concept.
[43] Bunge, 1967: 44-88.
[44] Bryant, 2010.

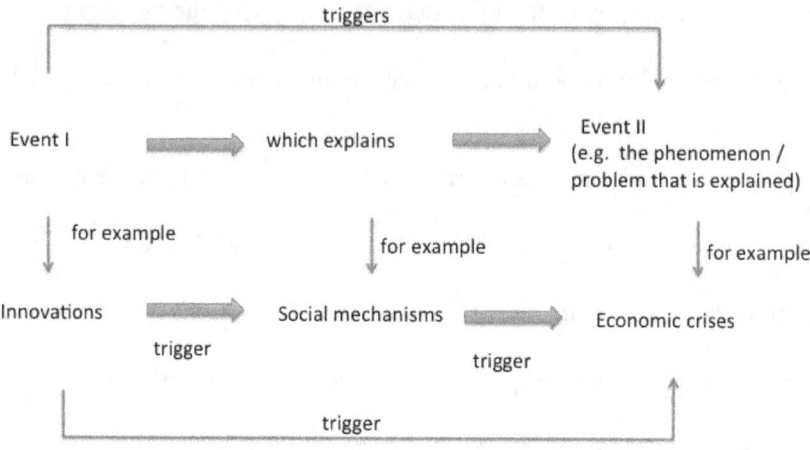

Case studies

Abercrombie et al. say the following: "…a case study cannot provide reliable information about the broader class […]"[45] Flyvbjerg comments that this statement is "indicative of the conventional wisdom of case-study research"[46], and there are a number of scientists who support this conventional knowledge that Abercrombie et al. advocate[47].

However, in the following I will present four exceptions to the general rule that one **cannot** "provide reliable information about the broader class."[48] I agree with Flyvbjerg's statement that "it is misleading to see

---

[45] Abercrombie et al., 1984:34.

[46] Flyvbjerg, 2006:220.

[47] Dogan & Pelassy, 1990:121; Diamond, 1996:6; Campbell & Stanley, 1966:6-7. Campbell adopted a different view at a later date, and realised the possibility of making generalisations from case studies (Campbell, 1975:179).

[48] Abercrombie et al., 1984:34.

the case study as a pilot method to be used only in preparing the real study's larger surveys, systematic hypotheses testing, and theory building."[49] Many scientists today consider case studies to be the most important method for developing knowledge[50]. My four exceptions to the general rule should not be confused with Flyvbjerg's, "Five Misunderstandings About Case-Study Research"[51]. Flyvbjerg and the author of this book deal with the same phenomenon but our perspectives are distinct, though our ideas concerning generalising from cases are similar.

Case studies provide the researcher with practical context-based knowledge, which may be seen in the research of, for instance, Freud, Marx, Darwin and Piaget. First, familiarity with the context may be developed in longitudinal case studies, and second, case studies where the researcher compares several cases over a period of time. In both these examples, it is reasonable to assume that it may be possible to generalise practical contextual knowledge, because familiarity with the context increases and access to different forms of knowledge also increases, because the researcher investigates over a long period within the context.

---

[49] Flyvbjerg, 2006:221.
[50] Campbell, 1975:178-191; Ragin & Becker, 1992; Lee, 1989; Wilson, 1987; Bailey, 1992; Griffins et al., 1991; Stake, 1995.
[51] Flyvbjerg, 2006:219-248.

Third, in specific parts of a case (such as where an innovative information and learning system is developed), it is reasonable to assume that lessons learnt can be transferred to other cases, both within the same industry and also to other industries[52]. Thus, innovation that occurs at one place in a social system can be transferred to other social systems[53].

Fourth and finally, generalisation can be made from case studies in relation to what may be termed "incidents". An incident in a case may concern a small intervention that is carried out by management, which proves to have considerable consequences. For instance, a case in which the management adopted a principle whereby the management were required to rationally and explicitly provide justifications concerning the rejection of any proposals made by employees; if justifications were not given, then the proposal would have to be implemented. The point being here is that a leader or manager cannot make decisions merely on the basis of their position of power within the hierarchy, but must examine proposals on the basis of rational and verifiable arguments. One such example appeared in a study carried out by Johannessen & Hauan, where the result was a productivity increase of 68 per cent in a particular section of a shipyard[54]. Such an incident has the potential to be

---

[52] Johannessen & Hauan, 1994:11-26.
[53] Rogers, 2003.
[54] Johannessen & Hauan, 1994:11-26.

generalised beyond the particular context.

Both incidents and specific parts of a case may be used to transfer experience. It is reasonable to assume that in such situations there is a potential for generalisation. The following proposition may be formulated: The greater the degree of innovation in *a specific part of a case study* and in *an incident*, the greater the likelihood generalisation can be carried out. Perhaps John Walton[55] makes a good point when he says that case studies produce the best theory!

Figure 5. Possible generalisations that can be made from a case study

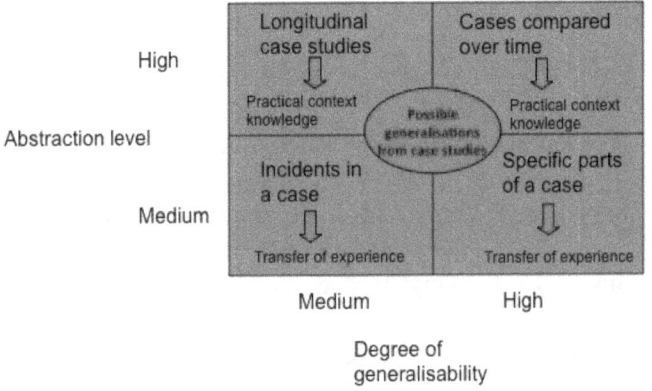

The above figure is based on the assumption that one can develop knowledge in a practical context, provided one is familiar with the context over a period of time. This insight also provides an

---

[55] Walton, 1992:129.

understanding of tacit knowledge and the various forms it can take[56].

Simply put, it may be said that longitudinal case studies and comparative case studies over time produce the best theories, because one becomes so familiar with the context that one is able to see Popper's "black swan" and refute the claim that "all swans are white"[57]. It is also possible to make a pointed formulation of incidents in a case study and specific parts of a case study: In these two modes it is possible to generalise from a sample which is less than one (1) (when the case = 1).

- ## Data mining models

"Data mining" models are based on large – often very large – datasets[58], the purpose being to identify possible structures and patterns in the data[59]. An attempt is made to extract information from the data set so that an understanding of relationships may be gained[60]. There is a small degree of abstraction in data mining models, but a very large amount of empirical material that is used[61]. Consequently, data mining models have a potential for higher levels of abstraction. The premise is, however, that

---

[56] Johannessen et al., 2001:3-20.
[57] Popper, 1959; 1963.
[58] Han, 2011.
[59] Witten et al., 2011.
[60] Bishop, 2007:500-654.
[61] Tan et al., 2013:234-435.

the concepts in the more abstract model must become freer of the context. If not, one could say that the data mining model creeps like a worm in the data. If this happens, the model does not have the ability to provide the necessary bird's eye view of the relationships and patterns.

It may be best to develop data mining models in three steps:

First, develop a data mining model based on a theory where propositions and hypotheses are developed.

Second, test these against the large amounts of data.

The third and final step is to visualise the relationships that emerge in the data.

However, this procedure is not so widely used in data mining[62]; it is more common to attempt to discover clusters in a large data set, and from these develop assumptions about relationships. Thus, from the clusters of data, information may be abstracted so that knowledge can be developed. The objection to this form of induction is that the researcher does not have familiarity with the data context, nor is he/she directed by a theory. This may result in an infinite number of interpretations in the pattern that emerges, although this need not be the case.

---

[62] Cf. Han, 2011; Witten, 2011; Bishop, 2007; Tan et al., 2013.

• A typology and strategy for the development of conceptual models

The conceptual models in Fig. 6, which have a high degree of abstraction, attempt to describe and explain the social landscape. This can be compared with a small-scale overview "map". The conceptual models in Fig. 7, which have a low level of abstraction, have a greater level of detail in their maps. The map metaphor is used deliberately, because maps of different scales have different applications. A small-scale overview map may be used to find out the general direction (or overview), whereas more detailed large scale maps may be used when someone wants to find their way, say, when walking over unknown terrain. However, it must be noted that a high degree of abstraction does not necessarily exclude the practical application of a conceptual model; also, a small degree of abstraction does not necessarily mean a model has a high degree of application. The degree of abstraction and the degree of generalisation is neither a one-to-one ratio, nor a linear relationship of other relationships. Conclusion I discusses the relationship between abstraction and generalisation.

Fig. 6 illustrates the schematic typology described above.

Figure 6. A schematic typology of conceptual models.

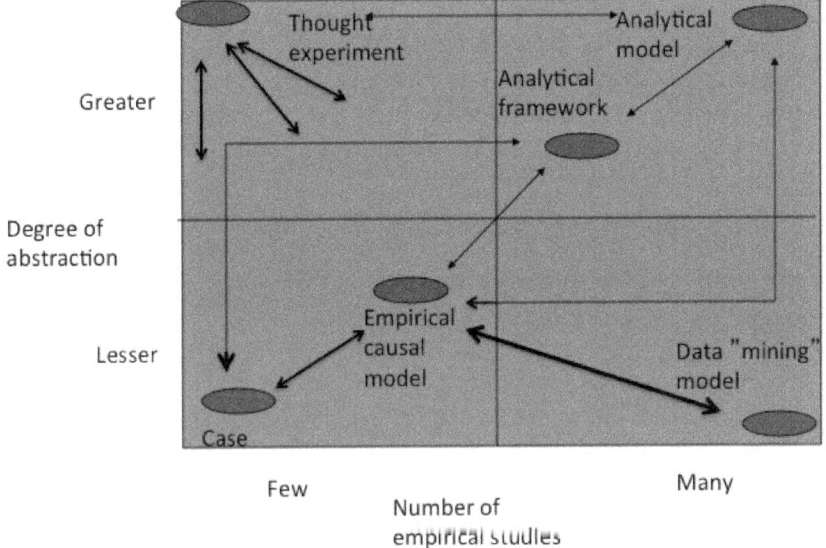

- ## A strategy for the development of conceptual models

What has been examined thus far may be summarised in the following points for the development of a strategy for designing conceptual models:

Clarify the problem/phenomenon.

Develop a precise research question.

Define the generic properties of the social universe that is being studied, and determine this in terms of various concepts, such as concepts A, B and C.

Determine the relations between the concepts, by using words such as 'influence', 'reinforce', etc.

Decide which components should be included in the concept.

Determine the key features of the components.

Develop indicators for the key features (cf. formal definition of

conceptual models, Part I).

Determine the relationships between the components of the various

concepts.

The eight points above represent the first step when developing

conceptual models. After this has been done, various strategies may be

followed. Points 9-13 provides an example of how to proceed further:

Construct an analytical framework (or thought experiment).

Develop an analytical model based on the analytical framework.

Use the analytical model to examine an empirical context.

Develop empirical causal models on the basis of the analysis from

point 11 and examine quantitatively an empirical context.

Develop and visualise the quantitative relationships emerging from t

he analysis in point 12.

Fig. 7 A strategy for developing conceptual models

High	Thought experiment	• Analytical scheme • Analytical model • Empirical causal model (based on large statistical studies)
Low	• Single case • Empirical causal model (based on small amount of data)	• Longitudinal case studies • Specific parts of a case study • Comparable cases over time • "Data mining"

Level of
abstraction

Lesser   Greater

Degree of generalisation

• Conclusion

The conclusion is divided into three parts. Conclusion I answers the

study question. Conclusion II deals with the study's practical

implications. Conclusion III looks at some theoretical implications of the

study.

Conclusion I: Answer to the study question

The study question is: How can we use conceptual generalisation in

social science?

The study has shown that there is diversity in conceptual models at

various levels of abstraction that may be used to a greater or lesser degree when giving advice in practical contexts.

A high degree of abstraction may be likened to a bird's eye view of a large geographical landscape in analogy to an overview map; thus, analytical models and analytical frameworks may be likened to globes, while the case studies may be likened to small scale maps of the type used when hiking. However, there is no one-to-one relationship between the degree of abstraction and the degree of generalisation. Case studies have, as a rule, a small degree of abstraction, but specific parts of a case study, such as the innovative new information and learning system[63] mentioned above, may have a large degree of generalisation. This learning system may be used to provide practical advice to many types of businesses, even outside the specific context of the industry in which the case study was carried out. We have also seen in Fig. 7 that it is not only specific parts of a case that can be generalised, but also longitudinal cases, comparative cases over time and incidents in case studies.

On the other hand, a thought experiment may have a high degree of abstraction, but does not have to be generalisable to a large extent; no practical advice needs to come from a thought experiment, though this is of course possible.

---

[63] Johannessen & Hauan, 1994.

Analytical schemes and analytical models have a high level of abstraction. In these, the possibility of considerable generalisation is also present, but not as a necessary consequence of abstraction. In other words, there is no linear causal relationship between abstraction and generalisation.

However, it is possible to say that there is a theoretical relationship between abstraction and generalisation. Turner and Boyn describe this theoretical relationship in the following way: "The more of reality to be examined, the more grand is the theory"[64]. However, the micro-macro link that Turner and Boyn refer to is not in focus here. Those interested in this approach may refer to Turner & Boyn[65], Alexander[66], Alexander et al.[67] and more recently Buskens & Raub[68], as well as Cetina & Cicourel[69].

Conclusion II: Practical implications

The first implication for research practice is that the researcher may acquire a more reflective approach to conceptual generalisation as a research strategy. Secondly, the researcher may use various types of

---

[64] Turner & Boyns, 2006:354.
[65] Turner & Boyns, 2006.
[66] Alexander, 1982.
[67] Alexander et al., 1986.
[68] Buskens & Raub, 2014.
[69] Cetina & Cicourel, 2014.

conceptual models at different levels of abstraction. Thirdly, the researcher may acquire a more reflective approach to the relationship between abstraction and generalisation. Fourthly, the researcher may more easily diagnose scientific studies based on the following criteria:

1. We diagnose problems that do not exist.

2. We do not diagnose problems that exist.

3. We may risk solving the wrong problem entirely correctly.

4. We may have the correct data, but we interpret it incorrectly.

5. We may risk not acting when we should have acted.

6. We may accidentally mistake correlation for causation.

7. We may risk focusing on what is correct, when we should have focused on avoiding what is incorrect.

Conclusion III: Theoretical implications

This study has shown that the various conceptual models may co-exist rather than compete with each other, and they may be used in the various contexts and niches of social reality. Sometimes this may concern processes at a micro level which are studied, while at other times it may concern processes at a macro level. It may also be the case that the researcher is searching for social mechanisms that reinforce a social

phenomenon. These social mechanisms may have implications at both

micro and macro levels. This may apply, for example, to the

phenomenon of economic crises. It is then possible to ask the following

question: What social mechanisms trigger, maintain and enhance

economic crises?

The difficulty of identifying social mechanisms, and distinguishing them

from processes, is, amongst other things, grounded in the fact that social

mechanisms are also processes[70]. In order to explain social mechanisms,

it is possible to utilise a Boudon-Coleman diagram, a research method

developed by Bunge[71]; he developed the diagram on the basis of insights

made by the sociologists Boudon and Coleman. The diagram he used

attempts to show the relationship between different levels, particularly

the macro- and micro levels. In the specific example he used, changes at

the macro level (technological innovations in semi-feudal systems) led to

increased income at the micro level (the income of the tenants); these

same changes led, however, to a weakening of semi-feudal structures

because the dependence of the tenants on land owners was reduced.

Consequently, the landowners opposed the changes, especially

---

[70] Bunge, 1997:414.
[71] Bunge, 1998: 76-79.

technological innovations (which Boudon had shown in his research)[72].

Coleman[73] started at the macro level, going down to the individual level to find explanations, and finally ended up at the macro level again. An important purpose of the diagram is to identify the social mechanisms that maintain or change the phenomenon or problem under investigation. In the case of Boudon's analysis of semi-feudal society, it was the social mechanisms (the technological innovations) that led to changes in the semi-feudal structures. The social mechanisms that hindered this were the land owners' fears that the tenants would become less dependent on them, as their income increased. In other words, Bunge's Boudon-Coleman diagram presents a "mixed strategy"[74], which he explains in his research strategy. He expresses this in the following way: "*When studying systems of any kind a) reduce them to their components (at some level) and the interaction among these, as well as among them and environmental items - but acknowledge and explain emergence whenever it occurs: and b) approach systems from all pertinent sides and on all relevant levels, integrating theories or even research fields whenever unidisciplinarity proves to be insufficient*"[75]. The purpose of this research strategy is to arrive at a deeper and more complete explanation

---

[72] Boudon, 1981:100.
[73] Coleman, 1990:7-12.
[74] Bunge, 1998:78.
[75] Bunge, 1998:78.

of the system's behaviour.

Fig. 8 Developing conceptual models at macro and micro levels

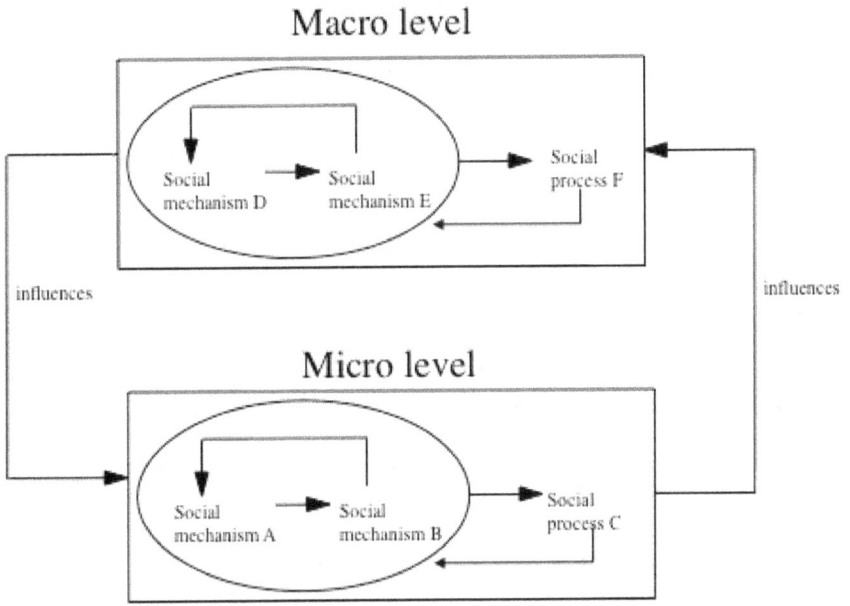

References

Abercrombie,N.; Hill, S. & Turner, B. (1984). Dictionary of Sociology, Penguin, Harmondsworth.

Ashby, W.R. (1945). Effect of Controls on Stability, Nature, vol.155,24. February.

Asplund, J. (1970). Om undran innfør samhället, Argos, Stockholm.

Asplund, J. (2010). Det sociala livets elementära former, Korpen, Stockholm

Bailey, K.D. (1990). Social Entropy Theory, State University New York Press, Albany.

Bailey, K.D. (1994). Sociology and the New Systems Theory: Towards a Theoretical Synthesis, State University of New York Press, Albany.

Bailey, K.D. (2006). Systems Theory, in Jonathan H. Turner, Handbook of Sociological Theory, Springer, New York. S. 379-405.

Bailey, M.T. (1992). Do Physicists Use Case Studies? Public Administration Review, 52, 1:47-54.

Bateson, G. (1972). Steps to an ecology of mind, Ballantine Books, New York.

Bateson, G. (1988). Ande och Natur, Symposion Bokförlag, Stockholm.

Beer, S. (1979). Heart of Enterprise, John Wiley & Son, New York.

Beer, S. (1985). Diagnosing systems for organizing, Prentice Hall, London.

Bishop, C.M. (2007). Pattern Recognition and machine Learning, Springer, Berlin.

Bryant, A. (2010). The SAGE Handbook of Grounded Theory, Sage, London.

Bunge, M. (1967). Scientific Research, Vol. 3, in studies of the foundations methodology and philosophy of science, Springer Verlag, Berlin.

Bunge, M.   (1974). Sense and Reference, Reidel, Dordrecht.

Bunge, M.   (1974a). Interpretation and Truth, Reidel, Dordrecht.

Bunge, M. (1977). Treatise on basic philosophy. Vol. 3. Ontology I: The furniture of the world. Dordrecht, Holland: D. Reidel.

Bunge, M.   (1979). A World of Systems, Reidel, Dordrecht.

Bunge, M. (1981). Scientific materialism. Boston, USA: D. Reidel.

Bunge, M. (1983). Exploring the World: Epistemology & Methodology I, Dordrecht: Reidel.

Bunge, M. (1983a). Understanding the World: Epistemology & Methodology II, Dordrecht: Reidel.

Bunge, M. (1985). Philosophy of Science and Technology. Part I: Epistemology & Methodology III, Dordrecht: Reidel.

Bunge, M. (1985a). Philosophy of Science and Technology. Part II: Epistemology & Methodology. Dordrecht: Reidel.

Bunge, M.   (1989). Ethics: The Good and the Right, Reidel, Dordrecht.

Bunge, M. (1989a). Treatise on basic philosophy. Vol. 8. Ethics: The good and the right. Dordrecht, Holland: D. Reidel.

Bunge, M. (1989b). Game theory is not a useful tool for the political scientist. Epistemologia, 12(1), 195–212.

Bunge, M. (1990). Boudon on anti-realism in social studies, I Weingartner,P. &

Dorn, G,J.W. Studies on Mario Bunges treatise, pp. 613-616, Rodopi, Amsterdam.

Bunge, M. (1995). The poverty of rational choice theory. In I. Jarvie & N. Laor (Eds.), Critical rationalism, metaphysics and sciences (Vol. 1, pp. 149–168). Dordrecht: Kluwer Academic Publishers.

Bunge, M. (1996). Finding philosophy in social science. New Haven: Yale University Press.

Bunge M. (1996a). The seven pillars of Popper′s social philosophy, Philosophy of the social sciences, 26, 4: 528-556.

Bunge, M. (1997). Mechanism and explanation. Philosophy of the Social Sciences 27: 410- 465.

Bunge, M. (1997a). Foundations of Biophilosophy, Springer Verlag, Berlin.

Bunge, M. (1998). Philosophy of science: From problem to theory, Volume one, Transaction Publishers, New Jersey.

Bunge, M. (1998a). Philosophy of science: From explanation to Justification, Volume Two, Transaction Publishers, New Jersey.

Bunge, M. (1998b). Social science under debate: A philosophical perspective. Toronto: University of Toronto Press.

Bunge, M. (1998c). Philosophy of science: From explanation to justification, Volume two, Transaction Publishers, New Jersey.

Bunge, M. (1999). The sociology-philosophy connection. New Brunswick, NJ: Transaction.

Bunge, M. (2000). Ten modes of individualism—none of which works—and their alternatives. Philosophy of the Social Sciences, 30(3), 384–406.

Bunge, M. (2001a). Philosophy in crisis: The need for reconstruction. Amherst, NY: Prometheus Books.

Bunge, M. (2001b). Rational choice theory: A critical look at its foundations. In M. Mahner (Ed.), Scientific realism: Selected essays of Mario Bunge (pp. 303–319). Amherst, NY: Prometheus Books.

Bunge, M. (2001c). Systems and emergence, rationality and imprecision, free-wheeling and evidence, science and ideology: Social science and its philosophy according to van den Berg. Philosophy of the Social Sciences, 31(3), 404–423.

Bunge, M. (2003). Emergence and convergence: Qualitative novelty and the unity of knowledge, University of Toronto Press, Toronto.

Bunge, M. (2006a). Chasing reality: Strife over realism. Toronto: University of Toronto Press.

Bunge, M. (2006b). A systemic perspective on crime. In P.-O. H.

Wikström & R. J. Sampson (Eds.), The explanation of crime: Context, mechanisms, and development (pp. 8–30). Cambridge: Cambridge University Press.

Bunge, M. (2007). Review of moral sentiments and material interests. Philosophy of the Social Sciences, 37(4), 543–547.

Bunge, M. (2009). Political philosophy: Fact, fiction and vision. New Brunswick, NJ: Transaction Publishers.

Bunge, M. (2010a). Matter and mind: A philosophical inquiry. New York: Springer.

Bunge, M. (2010b). Soziale Mechanismen und mechanismische Erkla¨ rungen. Berliner Journal für Soziol- ogie, 20, 371–381.

Bunge, M. (2014). Evaluating Philosophies, Springer, Berlin.

Bunge, M., & Ardila, R. (1987). Philosophy of psychology. New York: Springer-Verlag.

Campbell, D. T. (1975). Degrees of Freedom and the Case Study, Comparative Political Studies, 8, 1:178-191.

Campbell, D. T & Stanley, J. C. (1966). Experimental and Quasi-Experimental designs for research, Rand McNally, Chicago.

Deleuze, G. & Guattari, F. (2011). What is Philosophy, Verso, London.

Diamond, J. (1996). The Roots of Radicalism, The New York Review of Books, 14. November,pp. 4-6.

Dogan, M. & Pelassy, D. (1990). How to Compare Nations: Strategies in Comparative Politics, Chatam House, Chatham.

Einstein, A. (1936). Physics and Reality, J. Franklin Inst., 221:349-382

Elster, J. (2010). Explaining Social Behavior: More Nuts and Bolts for the Social Sciences", Cambridge University Press, Cambridge.

Facklam, M. & Johnson, P. (1992). Bee Dance and Whales Sing: The Mysteries of Animal Communication, Sierra Club. New York.

Feyerabend, P. (1993). Against Method, Verso, London.

Flyvbjerg, B. (2006). Five Misunderstandings about Case-Study Research, Qualitative Inquiry, vol. 12, 2:219-245.

Giddens, A. & Turner, J. (Eds.) (1987). Social Theory Today, Polity Press, Cambridge.

Griffins, L. J.; Botsko, C.; Wahl, A-M & Isaac, L.W. (1991). Theoretical Generality, Case Particularity, in Ragin, C. (Ed.) Issues and

Alternatives in Comparative Social Research, Brill, Leiden. S. 110-136.

Han, J. (2011). Data Mining: Concepts and Techniques, Morgan Kaufman, New York.

Homans, G.C. 81964). Bringing Men back in, American Sociological Review, 29:809-818.

Johannessen, J-A. & Hauan, A. (1994). Organizational Cybernetics: The Ecology of Change in a Norwegian Shipyard, Kybernetes, 23, 8:11-26.

Johannessen, J.-A. & J. Olaisen (2005). Systemic philosophy and the philosophy of social science-Part I: Transcendence of the naturalistic and the anti-naturalistic position in the philosophy of social science, Kybernetes Vol 34 No 7/8, 1261-1277.

Johannessen, J.-A. & J. Olaisen (2006). Systemic philosophy and the philosophy of social science-Part II: The systemic position, Kybernetes Vol 34 No 9/10, 1570-1586.

Johannessen, J.-A. & J. Olaisen (2006a). Hva er vitenskap? (What is Science?) Fagbokforlaget, Oslo.

Johannessen, J-A., Olaisen, J. & Olsen. B. (2001). Mismanagement of Tacit Knowledge: The Importance of Tacit Knowledge, the Danger of

Information Technology, and What to do about it? International Journal of Information Technology, 21, 1:3-20.

Kuhn, T. (2012). The Structure of Scientific Revolutions, University of Chicago Press, Chicago.

Lee, A.S. (1989). Case Studies as Natural Experiments, Human Relations, 42, 2: 117-137.

Luhmann, N. (1989). Ecological Communication, Polity Press, Cambridge.

Luhmann, N. (1995). Social Systems, Stanford University Press, Stanford.

Merton, R.K. (1957). The Role Set: Problems in Sociological Theory, British Journal of Sociology, 8:106-120.

Miller, J.G. (1978). Living Systems, McGraw Hill, New York.

Parson, T. (1951). The Social System, Free Press, Glencoe.

Popper, K. (1959). The Logic of Scientific Discovery, Basic Books, New York.

Popper, K. (1963). Conjectures and Refutations, Routledge, London.

Ragin, C. & Becker, H.S. (Eds.) (1992). What is a Case? Exploring the Foundations of Social Inquiry, Cambridge University Press, Cambridge.

Rhee, Y.P. (1982). The Breakdown of Authority Structure in Korea in 1960: A Systems Approach, Seoul National University Press, Seoul.

Rogers, E.M (2003). The Diffusion of Innovation, Simon & Schuster, New York.

Stake, R. (1995). The Art of Case Study Research, Sage, Thousand Oaks.

Tan, P-N.; Steinbach, M., Kumar, V. (2013). Introduction to Data Mining, Pearson, New York.

Tilly, C. (1998). Durable Inequality, University of California Press, Berkeley.

Turner, J. (1987). Analytical Theorizing, in Giddens, A & Turner, J. (eds.). Social Theory Today, Polity Press, Cambridge. S. 156-195.

Turner, J. (1988). A Theory of Social Interaction, Stanford University Press, Stanford.

Turner, J. (2002). Face to Face, Stanford University Press, Stanford.

Turner, J. (2007). Human Emotions, Routledge, London.

Turner, J. (2013). Human Institutions, Rowman & Littlefield, New York.

Walton, J. (1992). Making the Theoretical Case, in Ragin, C. & Becker, H. S. (eds.). What is a Case? Exploring the Foundations of Social Inquiry, Cambridge University Press. S. 121-137.

Wilson, B. (1987). Single-case Experimental Designs in Neuro-Psychological Rehabilitation, Journal of Clinical and Experimental Neuropsychology, 9, 5:527-544.

Witten, I.H.; Frank, E. & Hall, M. (2011). Data Mining, Morgan Kaufmann, New York.

Part II: Applications

Chapter 2: The use of distinction in the process of communication

• Introduction

The theoretical perspective of this chapter is systems theory, especially Luhmann´s perspective of communication (Luhmann, 1989; 1995; 2002). By theory we here mean, the system of propositions (Bunge, 1985).

The theory we develop is a generic one, i.e. it operates at micro, meso and macro level.

A social system's capacity for self-development depends largely on its capacity to communicate both internally and externally (Miller,1978). Without some level of communication, the system will very likely disintegrate (Maturama & Varela, 1980). Communication creates the idea of order, even where there is significant complexity and the system is bordering on chaos (Maturama, 1981).

When individuals, groups and organizations act and interact, their actions must encompass a greater realm of possibility than can be used by the surrounding environment. This is a simplified version of Ashby's law of requisite variety (Ashby, 2012). Ashby's law can also be described as a flexible response, i.e., social systems must be able to react at all times in such a way as to have a greater number of strategies available than is the case for the surrounding environment.

The aspect of our approach to the use of distinction in communication is our attempt to exploit the connections between the following three concepts: observation, differentiation and interpretation.

The system may be communicating at various levels, for example, individually, within groups or at an organizational level. The same three processes will operate at all three levels, is **our first assumption**.

Our second assumption is that functional differentiation (Knodt, 1995:xi) occurs continuously in dynamic social systems. The consequence of this is that functional differentiation is continuously giving rise to new distinctions (Luhman, 1995:30).

Our third assumption is that the use of distinctions can be applied to all phenomena/problems relating to social systems. The consequence of this is that distinctions are the fundamental component of all information and communications processes.

When we observe something new in a social system, we always observe differences, or as Bateson puts it: "the difference that makes a difference, is an idea." (Bateson, 1972:272). Such differences may be observed between the system and the surrounding environment, or between different functional differentiations. Luhmann subjects functional differentiation to a thorough theoretical examination (Luhmann, 1995). In fact, one of Luhmann's contributions to theoretical sociology may be described as his indication of the transition from structural functionalism to functional differentiation (Knodt, 1995:xi).

There is a distinction between linear and circular (interactive) explanatory models (Foerster, 1981; Bateson, 1972). Linear explanatory models may be likened to the billiard-ball model of causality, i.e. where one considers the cause and then the effect. Circular explanatory models are linked to communication systems, whereby the future, by means of a social mechanism based on the phenomenon of expectation, can be used to explain behaviour in the here and now (Weick, 1979). If one fails to distinguish between the linear and circular explanatory models, one may easily commit logical errors and misinterpretations. At worst, one may injure oneself, others and one's own ecosystem (Maturana & Varela, 1992; Cull, 2013).

The problem which is the foundation for this investigation is that complexity in communication makes the effective exchange of ideas difficult. The research question we examine is: **How can one use distinction in the process of communication to reduse complexity?**

The purpose is to improve the theoretical understanding of the communicative processes.

Fig. 1 sums up the introduction and shows how this article is structured.

Fig. 1 Philosophy of communication: Communication as process

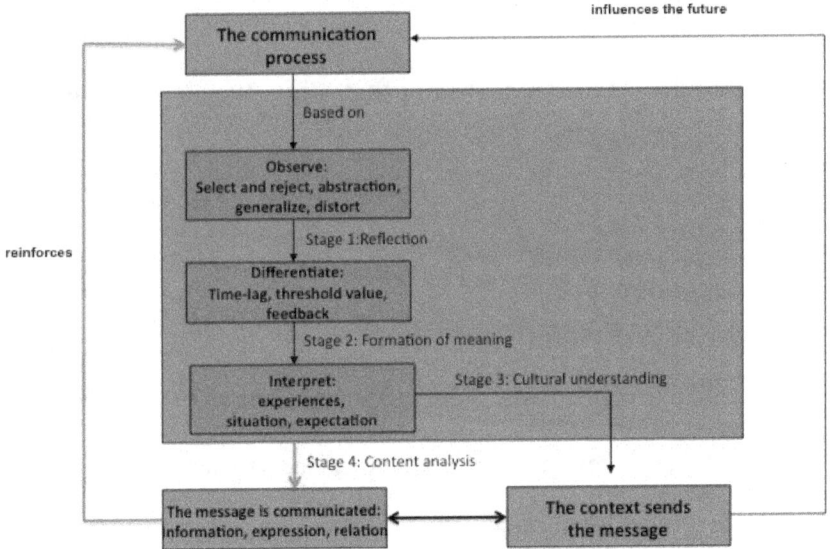

Observation

When we observe, we assume that we are doing this against the background of three main processes (Bateson, 1988:60; Maturana & Varela, 1992; Bandler & Grinder, 1982;1990):

1. We select something from a phenomenon or problem. Simultaneously, we decide to reject much of what is included in that phenomenon/problem-area.

2. We then apply processes of abstraction to make generalisations about what we have selected.

3. As these processes of abstraction take place, *the material that we have selected is transformed and distorted from its original form.* This idea is no more complex than the idea that data is different from information, which in turn is different from knowledge.

When we select and reject material from our observations, to a large extent we do this on the basis of our experiences (Bateson, 1988:60). Our experiences therefore guide us when we decide what we should select and focus on, in the here and now. It is also reasonable to assume that our experiences affect our expectations. If such a presupposition is correct, we may claim that our actions to a large extent are controlled by our experiences.

Proposition 1: The procedures for what we observe are based on our own fundamental experiences. It is these experiences that are determinative for our selection of some elements and our rejection of others.

Consequences: If our experiences collapse, for example, because of rapid changes in the surrounding environment, the manner in which we select some things within our perception while rejecting others will also be subject to change.

Observation may lead to spontaneous action, without progression through the stages of differentiation, interpretation and, finally, communication of a message. This point is considered by Luhmann (1995:300). According to Luhmann, this is precisely what happens in complex social situations, because the processes of observation and communication occur spontaneously (Luhmann, 1995:301-303). Because communication will take place more-or-less spontaneously in the aftermath of observation, one might envision that this is precisely what happens in crisis situations.

Proposition 2: In crisis situations, the communicative process is abbreviated to include only observation and then communication: the stages of distinction and interpretation are omitted.

Consequences: Communication in crisis situations is spontaneous, occurring without any process of reflection or opinion- forming.

When communication occurs in a crisis situation, one may envision that the reflective stage will take place after the communication of a message. Further, one may envision that this reflective stage will support an expectation about what one should do the next time a similar crisis occurs. Accordingly, the sequence of events is as shown in fig. 2.

Fig 2 Observation, communication, reflection

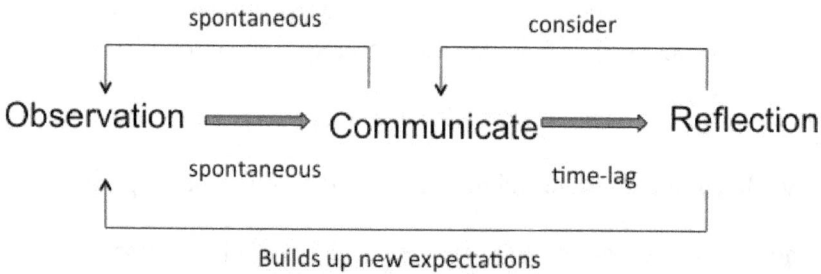

When reflecting on an action, one may obtain knowledge about the mistakes one made or the strategies by which one achieved success. This knowledge is then internalized as a kind of expectation that will be used in the new process of observation that one will conduct if a similar crisis occurs at a later date. The basic process, both in crises and in more ordinary situations, is that we select some things and thus reject others, we abstract and thereby distort what was our initial perception. Next time a similar incident occurs, we have internalized a process of reflection that will cause our spontaneous communication to be different from how it was on the previous occasion.

Proposition 3: Reflection is crucial to future communication processes.

Consequence: Without reflection, communication processes will degenerate into a situation where past errors are repeated.

Differentiation

We assume that differentiation takes place on the basis of three main processes (Bateson, 1972; Luhman, 2002; Foerster, 1981):

1. Time-lag is embedded.

2. There are complex feedback loops.

3. All phenomena and problems have a threshold value. If the

---

[76] Threshold values can also be exceeded, irreversible processes may be one part of the system can affect the threshold value at another place within the system. Systemic thresholds can also be triggered without an individual single threshold value being exceeded. However, threshold values may interact through complex feedback loops, so that they jointly exceed unforeseen threshold value and trigger irreversible consequences.

When differentiating, it is important to have a clear understanding of the three terms, feedback, time-lag and threshold value. The importance of feedback may be illustrated by the following example: what would happen if one puts one's hand on a glowing hot plate, and it takes ten minutes before the brain receives a signal of pain!? In the novel *Dead Souls* (1842) by the Ukrainian-Russian author Gogol, there is a description of what happens in a social system when there is a long time-lag in the communication of vital information; he describes how "dead souls" could be bought and sold as if they were financial assets. The "dead souls" were deceased serfs. Landlords received a subsidy for each serf, and they continued to receive the subsidy after a serf had died, because there was a considerable time-lag between the death of a serf and when the Moscow bureaucrats registered their deaths. Thus, in the time period between the serf's death and the registration of the death, the "dead soul" could be bought and sold. Similarly, "inside trading" may also represent a case where there is a time-lag in the communication of information. In this case, there is a time lag before certain information becomes public, thus giving "insiders" an advantage using non-public information which they can exploit when trading stocks.

In differentiating we constantly attempt to make comparisons. We even compare comparisons in an attempt to find patterns. We compare what we know with what we do not know. We compare what we believe to be facts with what the facts represent. We compare concepts to other concepts. We compile concepts in models and try to see if it may tell us something about what it is intended to represent. Comparisons are never objective, they are subjective. However, subjective perceptions can be tested against what they represent, i.e. subjective perceptions can be subjected to objective analysis through tests. Similarly, tacit knowledge can be objective in its consequences, even if it is subjective for the beholder of tacit knowledge.

Proposition 4: When we differentiate, we create differences.

Consequence: The most basic relationship between two variables in the communication world, factual or conceptual, is a difference (Bateson, 1972:130-134; 154-156; Bunge, 1983:164,Vol. 5. Differences are the basic unit of communication.

There are some conditions that must exist so that we are able to compare and create differences. These are the following; in analogy to Bateson's six criteria of mental processes (Bateson, 1988:134-135):

1. Comparisons must be made between two or more systems where the parts and the whole constitute an integrated system. The rationale is that comparisons can only be made within the same category, otherwise it is like comparing the word "fish" with an actual fish, and there is of course no resemblance between a fish and the word "fish".

2. Comparisons can only be made between systems that operate and are driven by differences. The rationale is that such systems operate in the communicative world, while systems in the natural world operate in relation to force and energy. If a distinction is not made between these two system categories, then logical errors may occur, culminating in errors of category.

3. Comparisons can only be made between systems that operate using interactive (circular) information processes, not linear. The rationale is that all systems in the communicative world are driven by interactive information processes, while processes in the natural world may often be understood linearly.

Proposition 5: Differences in communicating systems occur along two axes:

a. The axis: part-whole.

b. The axis where circular processes constitute a guiding principle.

Consequence: Differences create ideas, information, connections and patterns. Information and communication processes are driven by differences in the same way as an engine is driven by energy.

Interpretation

It is assumed that three processes are involved in interpretation (Luhman, 1995:59-103):

1. Our fundamental *experiences*.

2. The *context* in which the interpretation occurs.

3. To our *expectations*, providing guidelines for interpretation in the present.

Proposition 6: If our fundamental experiences change drastically, it is highly probable that our whole interpretation will also change.

Consequence: If our fundamental experiences collapse, the stability of our interpretations will also collapse.

When interpreting a distinction there are always two sides; this may be figuratively compared to a T-account, with left and right hand columns. When a person chooses to interpret one side of a distinction, then he/she rejects or de-emphasises the other side. This may be figuratively compared to tossing a coin – if the coin lands heads, the tails is still "involved" in the process even if it is the flipside (comparable to that which is rejected). In other words, the other side of distinction is still involved, although excluded from further interpretation, which in turn influences the communication of the message.

On the basis of such an understanding that one thinks using differences and distinctions, it can be assumed that the social world is interpreted from what is selected and rejected in relation to the distinction. Or to put it another way, it is possible to interpret the social world, and communicate this interpretation, precisely because there is something you choose not to interpret. Luhmann says: "Nothing can be observed (not even the nothing) without drawing a distinction."(Luhmann, 2002:87). This distinction, this boundary if you will, did not exist until an individual observed a problem or phenomenon and drew this distinction. The interpretation is thus a result of this highly personal and subjective demarcation or drawing of boundaries that creates a distinction. In this interpretation process something is selected and something is rejected; it creates an inside and an outside, where something is emphasised and something else is de-emphasised (Herbst, 2013:88).

Proposition 7: Interpretation is carried out by means of distinctions. **Consequence:** Each interpretation de-emphasises or rejects parts of the distinction.

Creating distinctions and interpretation is done, amongst others, on the basis of the fact that social systems maintain expectations (Luhmann, 1995:303). In this way, the distinctions that are created, and the interpretations that are made, are maintained through the norms and values that exist in the social system we are a part of.

When an observer creates a distinction, he/she simultaneously creates one or more meanings in relation to those who interpret the distinction, i.e. the distinction between tacit knowledge and explicit knowledge (Polanyi, 1983;Wagner, 1987). Meaning is thus a result of two processes. First, a distinction is created. Then the individual chooses to emphasise one side of the distinction and de-emphasise the other. Through these two processes meaning is developed. In this way, the observer frames in the phenomenon or problem in a certain way. This framing creates a dimension of interpretation that others have to relate to. As follows, the distinction gives the observer the power of interpretation, which can be utilised for various purposes. Whoever creates the distinction develops thereby meaning which is ascribed to the phenomenon or problem. The distinction thus becomes a marker, which creates a boundary. On one side of the boundary exists one reality; on the other side exists another. The meaning of the phenomenon/problem created by the individual is thus amplified by the fact that we develop our fundamental experiences through this process. Simultaneously, our expectations mechanism is also reinforced, i.e. how we should interpret similar situations in the future.

Proposition 8: Expectations guide the interpretation process.
Consequence: The development of meaning is reinforced by our expectations.

Similar to the physical limits imposed by national boundaries, it may be imagined what happens to the development of meaning when it is subjected to a de-limitation process. On one side of the boundary (i.e. distinction), one school of thought or meaning will emerge while a different school of thought/meaning will emerge on the other side. The boundary or limit in a distinction thus creates two completely different universes of thought/meaning. These schools of thought/meaning are created by the fact that there will always be some who choose to emphasise one side of the distinction that has been created, while others choose to emphasise the other side.

Distinction first creates a limit or a boundary; then it creates a dimension for interpretation. This dimension also provides guidance for action, which implies that the two schools of thought/meaning also interpret the actions of others differently.

The interpretation process similar to the observation process is a process of selection, i.e. we select something and reject something else. In addition, the outcome of the interpretation is also dependent on our experiences, the situation dynamics and our expectations. The provisional final result is that meaning is created. The interpretation is not a case of copying someone else's message or one's own observation and differentiation, but a creative process that creates meaning for the individual.

Proposition 9: Interpretation creates meaning.

Consequence: Gives the power of definition and power of defining models by creating meaning where apparent confusion prevails.

The message is communicated in a context which is part of a culture

When we observe, it is always done in a context. A context is the psychological framework of a situation, event, etc. (Bateson, 1972:186-187). Is it then possible to "see" a context? The context sends messages, Bateson writes (Bateson, 1972:185-187). To observe, differentiate and interpret in a context, one must be able to understand the signals transmitted by the context. Bateson refers to the psychological framework as meta-communication, that is, in order to "see" in the context we are in, we must understand the meta-communication. Culture may also be viewed as a meta-communication system. If the signals transmitted by the culture are not understood, it will be difficult to communicate in the context of which the individual is a part.

If the meta-communication is not understood, then paradoxes will easily arise. The occurrence of paradoxes in communicative contexts has a history of at least two thousand years; the paradoxes of the Greek philosopher Zeno (490-430 BCE)[77] (Zeno's paradoxes) are well known. Paradoxes are often divided into two categories, logical and rhetorical (Luhmann, 2002:80). Logical paradoxes should be avoided, while rhetorical paradoxes are used for various reasons. The Norwegian philosopher Zapffe formulated a paradox, Zapffe's Paradox: "It is that which you are good at that will be your downfall"[78]. Such rhetorical paradoxes provide a basis for reflection. For example, we are so good at technology that it is perhaps this which will be the destruction of mankind! In other words, rhetorical paradoxes are sentences and statements that contradict common sense. Paradoxes often create unexpected meaning that is contrary to assumed ideas (Luhmann, 2002:202, note 7).

Paradoxes may occur in communication when there are differences in the abstraction of logical types between communicating parties. This may lead to loss of meaning, but also to humour bringing the parties closer to each other (Bateson, 1972:187-189). Paradoxes can emerge between the

[77] http://en.wikipedia.org/wiki/Zeno_of_Elea

[78] https://en.wikipedia.org/wiki/Peter_Wessel_Zapffe

two sides in a distinction. Consider the Liar's Paradox, for example. In this case the two sides of the distinction are true-false. The paradoxical statement is as follows: "All Cretans are liars" (the utterer of the statement is also a Cretan). To solve a paradox of this type, one must establish acceptable conditions for the statement (Luhmann, 2002:88). The paradox has no conditions in itself and that is precisely why it is a paradox. In order to solve the Liar's Paradox it must be broken down into three conditions:

Statement 1: The utterer is from Crete. Condition C1

Statement 2: All Cretans are liars. Condition C2

Condition C3: C1 and C2 are disconnected.

When a paradox is unravelled in this way, it is no longer a paradox, but only two statements that are connected to conditions. The two statements above must then be verified empirically. Is the speaker from Crete? Is it true that all Cretans are liars? The probability that an infinite number of "black swans" will turn up in the empirical study are large, i.e., one quickly discovers that condition C2 is not true.

Proposition 10: Paradoxes in communication occur when the communicating parties operate at different levels of abstraction.

Consequence: Rhetorical paradoxes in communication can be overcome by breaking down statements in the paradox into clear conditions, which are then tested empirically.

Conclusion

Answer to the research question:

Research question: How can one use distinction in the process of communication to reduse complexity?

The answer is briefly formulated in the following: Distinction as a method consists of the main processes: observe, differentiate, and interpret (ODI).

Theoretical implications

Differences in the communication world may be explained in causal terms in relation to the billiard-ball model of causality in the physical world. Differences and ideas are created, inter alia, by a process that may be called punctuation (Bateson, 1972:271-273). Ideas are created, according to Bateson, precisely through "the difference which makes a difference"(Bateson, 1972:457). By punctuation a distinction is drawn between cause and effect; this is done with a clear motive in mind

(Bateson, 1972:292-293). A causality is thus created which does not actually exist in the real world, and one is then free to discuss the effects of this cause which has been created through a process of punctuation. A sequence of a process is selected, and then bracketed. In this way, we de-limit what is punctuated from the rest of the process. Figuratively, we may imagine this as a circle that is divided into small pieces; one piece of the circle is then selected and folded out into a straight line. This results in the creation of an artificial beginning and end (a circle obviously has neither beginning nor end). However, this relationship is created through punctuation for the purpose of appearing logical and consistent to an untrained observer. The premises are thus accepted and the observer falls into a communicative trap. In illustration, one can quote Ibsen's Peer Gynt: "The wilder the starting point, the result will oft be the more original"[79]

In distinction and punctuation, differences are introduced into the communication process. Distinction also creates a time dimension where expectation plays a role in interpretation. One acts, for example, often on the basis of what one expects from oneself and what one thinks others

[79] Dano-Norwegian: «Hvor utgangspunktet er galest, blir tidt resultatet originalest.» — Ibsen (*Peer Gynt*). Translation by William and Charles Archer. Alternative: Very often the oddest beginning, can lead to some really surprising results" (translator: Peter Watts).

expect you to do in the situation in question. Expectation is thus an important subset of the communication process, relating to a potential future where the future is also a part of the communication process.

Practical implications

The communication processes observation, differentiation and interpretation result in communication, bringing both past and future into the communication process. If there was no distinction between past and present, the individual (person A) would be able to present him/herself as he/she is in the present without considering the past. However, memory prevents the individual in question from presenting herself as she would like to be. Reactions from another person (person B) involve interpretations that take the individual's past into consideration, not only as they appear in the present. In this way, the communication processes, observation, differentiation and interpretation also create a connection between past and present, adding meaning to how the person "is," not only how he/she appears in the present. It may be said that history's "slow field" comes into play regarding the memory of the other, which becomes an important social mechanism for keeping person A firmly within an historic context. This context creates meaning, identity and coherence for person B in the communication process.

If the meeting between two people who have known each other is to be authentic, an effort must be made to forget what they know about each other. Of course this is in one sense impossible; therefore such a meeting will always be an encounter with the past. The individual is embedded within their culture and history, so that the presentation of himself/herself only constitutes a small thread of the whole.

Thus, memory functions as a very strong conservative characteristic in communication. One maintains perception of the other over time until differences impinge on what is perceived as their past. Even then an attempt will be made to reach further back in history within the culture in order to maintain our own perception. In other words, through the distinction process one keeps the other in an "iron cage" of memory, and will reluctantly release him/her.

The differences that the other presents over time must be differences that matter, i.e. "the difference which makes a difference,"(Bateson, 1971:271-273) and they must surpass some threshold value before we slowly begin to change our perception. It might be said in agreement with Bateson that our brains create images of the other, which we think we perceive (Bateson, 1988:55).

A common reaction when meeting new people, Bateson says, is to adopt assumptions characterised by suspicion, hostility and an authoritarian manner (Bateson, 1988:48-49). It may seem that one becomes unsure and confused when it is not possible to use experience and memory when meeting the other. Without communication's iron cage of memory one becomes confused and attempts to find other interpretative frameworks out of which one constructs "a cage", such as a person's geographical origin, their CV, their mode of dress, language, appearance, etc.

Theory Synopsis

Aspects of a communication theory

Assumption 1: Observation, differentiation and interpretation operates at various levels.

Consequence: The three processes creates distinctions in and between levels.

Assumption 2: Functional differentiation occurs continually in dynamic social systems.

Consequence : Functional differentiation continually creates new distinctions.

Assumption 3: Distinction as a method is applicable to all phenomena / problems in social systems.

Consequence : Distinctions are the basic unit of information and communication processes.

Observation

Proposition 1: The procedures for what we observe are based on our own fundamental experiences. It is these experiences that are determinative for our selection of some things and our rejection of others[80].

 Consequences: If experiences collapse, for example because of rapid changes in the surrounding environment, the manner in which we select some things within our perception while rejecting others will also be subject to change.

Proposition 2: In crisis situations, the communicative process is abbreviated to include only observation and then communication: the stages of distinction and interpretation are omitted.

Consequences: Communication in crisis situations is spontaneous, occurring without any process of reflection or forming of opinion

---

[80] Bateson, 1988:60.

Proposition 3: Reflection is crucial to future communication processes.

Consequence: Without reflection, communication processes will degenerate into a situation where past errors are repeated.

Differentiation

Proposition 4: When we differentiate, we create differences.

Consequence: The most basic relationship between two variables in the communication world, factual or conceptual, is a difference. [81] Differences are the basic unit of communication.

Proposition 5: Differences in communicating systems occur along two axes:

    a. The axis part-whole.

    b. The axis where circular processes constitute a guiding principle.

Consequence: Differences create ideas, information, connections and patterns. Information and communication processes are driven by differences in the same way as an engine is driven by energy.

Interpretation

---

[81] Bunge, 1983:164 (Volume 5); Bateson, 1972:130-134; 154-156.

Proposition 6: If our fundamental experiences change drastically, it is highly probable that our whole interpretation will also change.

Consequence: If our fundamental experiences collapse, the stability of our interpretations will also collapse.

Proposition 7: Interpretation is carried out by means of distinctions.

Consequence: Each interpretation de-emphasises or rejects part of the distinction.

Proposition 8: Expectations guide the interpretation process.

Consequence: The development of meaning is reinforced by our expectations.

Proposition 9: Interpretation creates meaning.

Consequence: Gives the power of definition and power of defining models by creating meaning where apparent confusion prevails.

Proposition 10: Paradoxes in communication occur when the communicating parties operate at different levels of abstraction.

Consequence: Rhetorical paradoxes in communication can be overcome by breaking down statements in the paradox into clear conditions, which are then tested empirically.

References

Adriaenssen, D. & Johannessen, J-A. (2015). Conceptual

generalisation:

Methodological reflections in social science a systemic viewpoint,

Kybernetes, 44, 4: 588-605.

Ashby, W.R. (2012). An Introduction to Cybernetics, Filiquarian

Legacy Publishing, New York.

Bandler, R. & Grinder, J. (1982). Reframing, Real People Press,

Moab, Utah.

Bandler, R. & Grinder, J. (1990). Frogs Into Princes, Real People

Press, Moab, Utah.

Bateson, G. (1972). Steps to an ecology of mind, Ballantine Books,

New York.

Bateson, G. (1988). Ande och Natur, Symposion Bokförlag,

Stockholm.

Bunge, M. (1983). Exploring the World: Epistemology & Methodology

I, Dordrecht: Reidel.

Bunge, M. (1983a). Understanding the World: Epistemology & Methodology II, Dordrecht: Reidel.

Bunge, M. (1985). Philosophy of Science and Technology. Part I: Epistemology & Methodology III, Dordrecht: Reidel.

Bunge, M. (1998). Philosophy of science: From problem to theory, Volume one, Transaction Publishers, New Jersey.

Bunge, M. (1999). Dictionary of Philosophy, Prometheus Books, Amherst, New York.

Cull, J. (2013). Living Systems: An Introduction to the Theories of Humberto Maturama and Francisco Varela, Create Space, New York.

Foerster, H, von (1981). Observing Systems, Intersystems Publications, Seaside, CA.

Herbst, P. G. (2013). Alternatives to Hierarchies, Springer, Berlin.

Hirschmann, A.O. (1990). Exit, Voice and Loyalty: Responses to Decline in Firms, Organizations and States, Harvard University Press, Boston.

Knodt, E.M. (1995) Foreword, in Luhmann, N., Social Systems, Stanford University Press, Stanford. pp. Ix-xxxvi.

Luhmann, N. (1989). Ecological Communication, Polity Press, Cambridge.

Luhmann, N. (1995). Social Systems, Stanford University Press, Stanford.

Luhmann, N. (2002). Theories of Distinction, Stanford University Press, Stanford.

Maturama, H. (1981). Autopoiesis, in Zeleny, M. (Ed.). Autopoiesis, Elsevier, London. pp. 21-33.

Maturana, H. & Varela,F. (1980). Autopoiesis and cognition, Reidel, Dordrecht.

Maturama, H. & Varela, F. (1992). Tree of Knowledge, Shambhala, New York.

Miller, J.G. (1978). Living Systems, McGraw-Hill, New York.

Polanyi, M. (1983). The tacit dimension, Gloucester, Mass.

Wagner, R.K. (1987). Tacit knowledge in everyday intelligent behavior, Journal of Personality and Social Psychology, 52: 1236-1247.

Weick, K.E. (1979). The Social Psychology of Organizing".2.nd. ed., Addison

Wesley Publishing Company, London.

Withey, M. and Cooper, W.H. (1989). Predicting exit, voice, loyality

and neglect. Administrative Science Quarterly, 34: 521-539.

Chapter 3 A general research methodology

Introduction

Our aim in writing this article has been the wish to help social scientists who study social systems from a systemic point of view. It is to position systemic thinking in the form of a general scientific methodology this chapter has as its main purpose, and this is also the contribution of the chapter. The purpose is also to facilitate the work of researchers studying problems/phenomena in social systems from a systemic point of view (Johannessen & Olaissen, 2005; 2005a)

Our basis for the study is Bunge`s systemic philosophy (Bunge, 1977; 1981; 1983; 1983a; 1985; 1985a; 1989; 1996; 2001). Mario Bunge is today one of the few system philosophers still active, to base his philosophy on a systemic foundation. One of the other few is Nicholas Rescher, whose conceptual idealism forms an interesting antonym to Bunge`s thinking,

The core of systemic thinking is to acquire insight into connections and patterns, and it provides and alternative to both individualism and holism

(Bunge, 1996:44).

Understanding, explanation and predication (wherever possible) will, as far as systemic thinking is concerned, always be oriented towards deeper contexts and therefore the construction of new patterns. It is the pattern which combines (Bateson, 1972) systemic thinkers always are looking for dealing with scientific problems/phenomena. It is the construction and synthesis that constitute the search object. The analysis is purely a tool in order to reach it. If the analysis is given precedence, the construction and synthesis will lag behind. Science is for systemic thinking a moral project (Bunge, 1989; Johannessen, 1997b). If science is not constructed as a moral project, it will not only lose its legitimacy, but also its direction, which is the search for truth, and can thus be a means to achieve unethical goals.

The systemic approach is based on a system-theoretical ontology, where the world is seen as a system consisting of subsystems, and an epistemology combining realism and rationalism. The aim of the systemic approach is to understand, predict, and control. The methods include analysis as well as synthesis, generalisation and systematisation (Johannessen, 1996; 1997; 1997a;).

The systemic position makes a distinction between the epistemological sphere (Bunge, 1985), the ontological sphere (Bunge, 1983), the axiological sphere (Bunge, 1989; 1996) and the ethical sphere (Bunge, 1989).

The conceptions held by a neutral observer on social systems would influence his acts, even if his conceptions are wrong or true. Systemic investigations therefore start "from individuals embedded in a society that pre-exists them and watch how their actions affect society and alter it" (Bunge, 1996:241). The study of social systems from a systemic perspective for this reason always include the triad: actors, observers, social systems. The observer tries to disclose the objective composition, environment and structure (CES) of a social system, then the subjective notion the actors have of CES. Furthermore we are interested in the mental models actors have of the social system, and the mental models we as observers have of the same system. It is then both subjective and objective aspects that need to be studied. When studying changes in the social system, which is the subject matter of cybernetics, we must from a systemic point of view investigate the social mechanisms influencing the changes. It is the internal and external social mechanisms that need to be disclosed within the political, economical, the cultural and the social ., in addition to the relations between the partial systems.

The first decision a researcher must take is to determine what is to be studied, i.e. the unit of analysis (individual, group, organisation, society i.e.). But any analysis is part of or embedded in a larger system. Therefore it is important in systemic thinking always to see the unit of analysis in the light of a larger system which it is part of, in order to understand the function, role, etc. it has in the larger system. Then it must be investigated how the unit of analysis is embedded in the system level underneath, in order to understand which function, role, etc. the analysis has in relation to this system.

The problem question of the article is: **How can we develop a general scientific methodology, on tenets from Mario Bunges philosophy?**

Five research questions have been developed in order to attempt to answer the problem question:

Q1: What demands must a general scientific methodology meet?

Q2: What assumptions are a general scientific methodology based on?

Q3: How are problems and problem questions developed in a general scientific methodology?

Q4: How does a general scientific methodology relate to hypotheses in scientific studies?

Q5: How does a general scientific methodology relate to theory in scientific studies?

The above description is summarised in Fig. 1, which also shows how the article is organised.

Fig. 1 A general scientific methodology on tenets from Mario Bunge's philosophy of social science

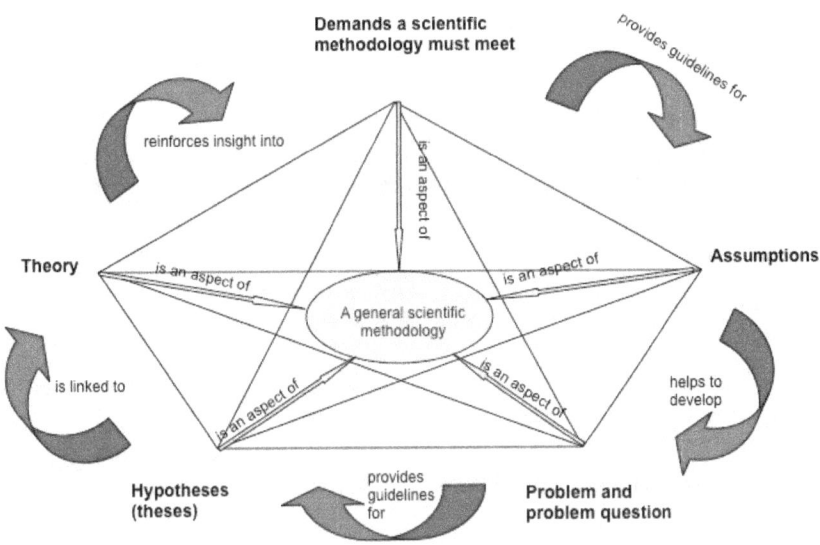

The demands that a general research methodology must meet

The following question will be examined here: What demands must a general scientific methodology meet?

There are two main categories of scientific methodology: **general scientific methodology and specific scientific methodology.** The general scientific methodology is of the following form: Problem or phenomenon, problem definition, problem question, research questions (hypotheses), literature review (theory), model, research, findings, explanation. There are various procedures for each step in general scientific methodology.

Most students are drilled in specific scientific methodology, which is divided into quantitative and qualitative methods. To master the production of scientific knowledge researchers should be specialists in general **and** specific methodology; he/she must use various specific methods in their scientific production to become familiar with different ways of developing knowledge. Familiarity with general methodology, however, is a prerequisite for all procedures in specific methodology.

In the systemic perspective, general scientific methodology constitutes the basic platform which all the subordinate concrete methods must relate to (Bunge, 1998; 1998a). Being adept at using specific scientific methodology, but not well versed in the use of general scientific methodology, may be likened to having a boat with a rotten hull but a very good engine.

---

[82] The five criteria are reduced from Bunge's initial ten criteria for establishing a scientific methodology (Bunge, 1983: 253-254, Volume 5); this has been done for pedagogical reasons, hopefully while still retaining scientific rigour.

A scientific methodology has as a minimum the following five characteristics (Bunge, 1983:253-254)[82]; they are logically organised by

the process of the scientific study.

1. **(E):** Data, information and knowledge collected using the
   methodology must be able to **explain** at least some aspects
   of the phenomenon or problem being studied.

2. **(A):** The methodology will be used to **analyse** data,
   information and knowledge that emerges in the study.

3. **(V):** The results and the procedure must be **verifiable** by
   others who have knowledge of the methodology. The
   verifiability must be able to determine whether **the results**
   are true within a given deviation.

4. **(C):** The results obtained using the methodology should be
   **criticised by researchers with knowledge of the
   methodology:**

[83] Researchers stand divided with regard to various scientific-theoretical and *scientific-philosophical* ideas. This means that there will always be some researchers who disagree with the appropriateness or validity of the chosen methodology. However, such disagreements are usually based on basic science and philosophical foundations, such as phenomenology, hermeneutics, logical empiricism, and to a lesser degree, the functionality of the methodology.

5. **(Rc):** The **research community** should be familiar with the methodology (and possibly have developed it) and have received specialized training in the use of it. New methodology should not be used until it has been tested by a research community[83].

The demands that a scientific methodology based on conceptual generalizationin must meet can thus be written: **(E, A, V, C) + (Rc)**

Assumptions

The question we will investigate is the following: What assumptions are a general scientific methodology based on?

All research is based on explicit and implicit assumptions. The following presents an example of a **logical assumption**: if one assumes that the work environment affects productivity in an organization, then it would make sense to implement measures to improve the working environment. This is called linear thinking, because it literally occurs in a line from cause to effect - in this case, the work environment and productivity. If, however, one assumes that the work environment affects productivity, but also that productivity affects the work environment, then it is **not** obvious how to implement measures to improve productivity. For instance, measures could be implemented to improve productivity by introducing new technology. If this resulted in increased productivity, it could be assumed in this line of thinking that the work environment would also be improved, because productivity affects the work environment. This latter way of thinking is called circular thinking (or interactive thinking)(Bateson, 1972). Since a circle has no beginning or end, this approach means that whatever the starting point, the end result will be the same. The two ways of thinking may be explicit to some people but less than explicit to others, and in some cases they will not be explicit at all but implicit or hidden. The systemic perspective is based on circular or interactive understanding of relationships (Bunge, 1998; 1999).

Assumptions may also be ontological. An example of an **ontological assumption** is that social facts exist, which is also characteristic of a systemic perspective. It is important in this context to distinguish between social facts and mental constructs of these facts. Example: Hunger is a social fact, but social distress is a mental construct.

Another ontological assumption is that a system at a higher level has properties that a system at a lower level does not have. This assumption relates to emergence.

Emergence is an important concept in systemic thinking. An emergent is if something new occurs on one level that has not previously existed on the level below. By emergent we mean here: *"Let S be a system with composition A, i.e. the various components in addition to the way they are composed. If P is a property of S, P is emergent with regard to A, if and only if no components in A possess P; otherwise P is to be regarded as a resulting property with regards to A."* (Bunge, 1977:97).

The assumption in other words is that emergent properties occur at a higher system level. Economic growth, for instance, is a property that does not exist at the individual level, but at organisational and social levels. Social mobility and political stability are similar examples. For instance, a social function has no meaning without viewing it in relation to other social functions in a system. Functional differentiation is thus a property of a system which is not found at the individual level.

Methodological assumptions relate to issues concerning scientific process and procedure.
The view that individuals (actors) are the only active people in a social system is called individualism, or (by some) methodological individualism.

Methodological individualism, possibly the most widespread of rationalist doctrines, states that social phenomena should be explained in terms of *"the psychologies and situations of the participants in these situations"*(Miller, 1978:387). The doctrine may be expressed as follows: Facts about social systems must be explained by facts about the individuals that constitute such systems. Methodological individualism *"claims that the understanding of social facts requires only the investigation of the beliefs, intentions, and actions of the individual concerned."(Bunge, 1996:249)*. It may be said that methodological individualism attempts to explain the whole by referring to the parts.

Methodological collectivism, on the other hand, attempts to explain the behaviour of the parts by referring to the whole. This represents the opposite position to methodological individualism.

The systemic perspective in social science attempts to make a connection between methodological individualism and methodological collectivism. Structure and organisation are such collective phenomena. Individuals who act are individual phenomena. A systemic perspective takes all these perspectives into account.

An **epistemological assumption** is based on understanding of how knowledge processes are developed. We will consider here the two central epistemological assumptions in a systemic perspective: social laws and social mechanisms.

When a hypothesis is well documented over time, a pattern can be established - some would say a **social law**. In the social sciences, social laws are controversial; hence we will briefly clarify what is meant by this construct in a systemic perspective.

Social laws constitute a pattern of a unique type. They are systemic and connected to a system of knowledge, and cannot change without the facts they represent also being changed (Bunge ,1983; 1983a). The main differences between a statement of a law and other statements are:

1. Law statements are general.

2. Law statements are systemic, i.e. they are related to the established system of knowledge.

3. Law statements have been verified through empirical studies.

A pattern may be understood as variables that are stable over a specific period of time. A social law is created when an observer gains insight into the pattern. By gaining such insight, we can also predict parts of behaviour or at least develop a rough estimate within a short period of time.

Social laws are further related to specific social systems, both in time and space. However, this does not represent any objection to social laws, because this is also true of natural laws (although these have a longer time span and are of a more general nature).

A social mechanism is also an epistemological assumption in a systemic perspective (but not only for this perspective). Bunge says: *"...a (social) mechanism is a process in a concrete system, such that it is capable of being about or preventing some change in the system as a whole or in some of its subsystems"* (Bunge, 1997:414). By social mechanism we mean those activities that promote or inhibit social processes in relation to a specific problem or phenomenon.

It is one thing to indicate relationships between phenomena, but something quite different to give satisfactory explanations of these relationships. It is the latter which a social mechanism should do. A social mechanism tells us what will happen, how it will happen and why it will happen (Bunge, 1967). Social mechanisms are primarily analytical constructs, which cannot necessarily be observed: they are, however, observable in their consequences. An intention may be considered to be a social mechanism of action. Although we cannot observe intent, we can interpret it in the light of the consequences that are manifested through action. Preferences may also be considered to be a social mechanism of economic and organizational behaviour; although we cannot observe people's preferences, we can interpret them in light of the behavioural consequences which they manifest. Understood in this way, social mechanisms are analytical constructs that indicate relationships between events (Hernes, 1998).

Material resources and technology are social mechanisms of the economic subsystem, power is a social mechanism of the political subsystem, fundamental values are a social mechanism of the cultural subsystem, and human relationships are a social mechanism of the social subsystem. These system-specific social mechanisms interact with each other to achieve certain goals, maintain these systems, or to avoid certain undesirable conditions in the system or the outside world. The difficulty of discovering social mechanisms and distinguishing them from processes may be partly explained by the fact that social mechanisms are also processes (Bunge, 1997:414).

Problem and problem question

The question that will be examined here is the following: How are problems and problem questions developed in a general scientific methodology?

The problem question should satisfy at least two criteria:

1. Firstly, it should as a rule be useful in a practical context. This is the

pragmatic test of the problem question.

2. Secondly, it should be related to existing knowledge. This is the knowledge test of the problem question.

Similarly, the conclusion or answer to the problem question should also be subjected to similar tests:

1. What are the practical implications of the findings? For instance, will they be of use to a leader involved in a process of change?

2. What are the theoretical implications of the findings? In other words, how do they relate to existing knowledge - do they support it or not?

Problem

Scientific problems may be empirical and conceptual. Empirical problems are related to a data base, which can be analysed. Conceptual problems do not presuppose a data base, but rather a knowledge base.

The systemic approach to defining and solving a problem is that it consists of three main parts (Bunge, 1985a): The problem's prerequisites, the processes that are involved in solving the problem and the solution(s).

The three parts have three related questions:

1. What is the history of the problem?
2. Which actors are interested in the problem remaining a problem?
3. Which solutions will ensure the problem is not solved in such a way that it creates new unwanted problems in the future?

If we respond satisfactorily to these three questions, we will have to a great extent set the limits of the actions we will later carry out when solving the problem.

There are three main types of problem that the systemic perspective is concerned with (Bunge, 1983):

- Why-problems. For example: Why do the employees in department X experience central override as a major problem in the change processes they are involved in?

- What-if problems. For example: What happens in an organization if the fear of inadequacy spreads in a change process?

- Real existing problems. For example: Are there groups in your organisation that actively oppose change?

It is always easier to describe a problem (a real existing problem) than to *explain* why the problem occurred (*why-problem*). We need both these approaches because a description of a problem must be available before we can explain it.

When we are faced with a problem, we first seek information. We may ask the question. *What* is the problem? Then we try to arrive at a description of the problem: *How* has the problem developed and evolved? What consequences arise as a result of this particular problem? Finally, we are interested in explaining the problem. Then we ask the question: *Why* is there a problem? The purpose of the explanation is that it will provide guidelines for the solution of the problem.

What constitutes an explanation of a problem? Problems may be understood in different ways and to varying degrees, but they must be understood adequately before they can be explained. Regardless of how we proceed when explaining a problem, it is important that the problem is systemised, perhaps into a main problem and associated sub-problems. Consequently, it becomes easier to understand what is the main problem and how some sub-problems are related to it.

When explaining a problem at least five types of explanation are used:

1. Those that indicate a cause and effect relationship.

2. Those that indicate a random event as a cause of the problem.

3. Those that indicate an interaction between various, interrelated forces.

4. Those that refer to conflicts between persons or groups as driving forces of a problem's development.

5. Those who show that the problem is related to the goals that the system has set.

The problem question and research questions

When the problem is analysed the next step in a systemic investigation is to develop the problem question. The problem question is formulated always as a question related to the problem that has been analysed. As a rule, the problem question is an overarching one and only operational to a small extent, such as: What promotes and inhibits organizational innovation? It is impossible to say anything sensible about such an overarching question. Therefore, the problem question must be broken down into a number of research questions (for instance, 3 to 5 questions).

Research questions are always operational, so it is possible to answer them using various concrete scientific methods, which may be of different types. Simplified, one can say that the research questions constitute the system that constitutes the problem question; thus, they are the parts that together constitute the problem question. The problem question is only one of many approaches (perhaps infinitely many) that may be constructed in relation to the problem being analysed. As explained above, it's the problem analysis that is essential, then the design of a precise problem question. Finally, research questions are developed that can be operationalised using some indicators and recognized methods.

Hypotheses

The following question will be examined: How does a general scientific methodology relate to hypotheses in scientific studies?

To answer the question, first phenomenological and dynamic hypotheses will be discussed, and then indicators.

Phenomenological and dynamic hypotheses

Hypotheses are intended to act as a link between our mental and social constructs, on the one hand, and social facts on the other (Turner, 1988; 1991). For instance, hunger is a social fact, while social deprivation is not a fact but rather a mental or social construct. Not being able to read is a social fact, while illiteracy is a social construct. Mixing up mental and social constructs and what these are meant to represent creates confusion and should be avoided.

Hypotheses are intended to provide explanations of social facts or to reveal correlations between social facts. The first is called dynamic hypotheses and the latter phenomenological hypotheses (Bunge, 1983a).

It is always easier to describe a condition or a change in a state (phenomenological hypotheses) than to explain how and why the condition or change developed (dynamic hypotheses).
Examples of phenomenological hypotheses:

a) The more external information an organisation uses, the more likely it is that it will achieve its goals.

b) The more communication channels there are to the leadership in an organisation, the more likely it is that the quality of the work environment will be better.

Examples of dynamic hypotheses:

1. The more external information an organisation uses, the more likely it will achieve its goals, **because** uncertainty is reduced.

2. The more communication channels there are to the leadership in an organisation, the more likely the quality of the work environment will be better, **because** the leadership will be able to intervene quickly and decisively to change poor work environment conditions.

Both types of hypotheses are necessary because a description of/change in a condition must be available before we can attempt to explain why such a condition has arisen.

Dynamic hypotheses are preferable to phenomenological hypotheses in a systemic perspective because the former include an element of explanation. In most cases, research attempts to provide explanations of a problem or a phenomenon (Bunge, 1985; 1985a).

In order for a hypothesis to be realised (not proven), three criteria must be met (Bunge, 1985):

- Variables must correlate.

- The causal direction must be made visible.

- There must be no other variables which in some way have an effect that cannot be made visible.

All types of hypotheses have to meet three demands. Firstly, of two competing hypotheses, we should prefer the one that is best rooted in practice. Secondly, we should prefer the hypotheses that are rooted in existing knowledge. Thirdly, we also need to consider the systemic nature of hypotheses, that is, whether they are rooted in a theory. In a well-developed science, systemic hypotheses are to be preferred.

Indicators

Indicators are essential so that the researcher is able to come to grips with the problem or phenomenon being examined. What is an indicator? Let us take an example from the field of medicine. Fever is an indicator of an underlying disease, but it does not tell us what disease is causing the fever. By this example, it may be said that an indicator is an observable variable. The variable can be observed directly or indirectly by using an instrument that signals something about the variable being investigated (the variable in the above example cannot be observed directly).

Unemployment may be said to be an indicator of various underlying phenomena and problems. For instance, it may be caused by a low level of education, but it can also be caused by types of higher education that are not in demand. Unemployment may also be caused by technological innovations. Poverty may also be a cause of unemployment because malnutrition and a lack of education can result in the population being unable to adapt to the labour market. However, unemployment is usually considered in the context of reduced economic growth. The point being made here is that unemployment can be an indicator of one or more underlying phenomena, but which ones? To clarify the relationships we often need a theory that shows relationships between indicators and the phenomenon under investigation.

Indicators can be quantitative, such as a basal thermometer used for measuring body temperature in cases of suspected fever. Quantitative indicators are often considered to be valid and objective. Figures, number, quantity and volume are examples of types of quantitative indicators. Indicators may also be qualitative, such as the degree of exercise of power in an organisation, the degree of bureaucracy in an organisation, etc. Qualitative indicators are sometimes considered to be subjective and unreliable, because they depend on interpretations and personal assessments relating to the use of the indicator. However, qualitative indicators are of interest when people's perceptions, expectations and assumptions about future situations are important.

In addition to the fact that indicators can be quantitative and qualitative, they can also be empirical and theoretical. An example of an empirical indicator is inequality in the distribution of value creation (the Gini coefficient). Some indicators, however, are theoretical. An example of a theoretical indicator in economics is price elasticity. This indicator (I) tells us something about the percentage change of the price (P) when there occurs a percentage change in quantity demanded (E) ($I = (E / P)$).

Theory

The following question will be examined: How does a general scientific methodology relate to theory in scientific studies?

Any field of study starts out with a problem/phenomenon, a data basis, the search for relevant variables and the construction of hypotheses/theses or research questions. As research progresses, stronger relationships will be developed between the hypotheses. New hypotheses are developed, and as a result, a system of hypotheses is constructed. When a field of study has developed a system of hypotheses, we say that a theory has been developed. In the systemic perspective, a theory is defined as a system of propositions (Bunge, 1985).

Propositions are overarching hypotheses.

The development of a field of study to a science will always follow a path in which data and hypotheses are systemised and structured into a system of hypotheses. When this happens, the hypotheses will become supported by a continually developing knowledge base, and the goal is the development of a theory.

Theory development in a systemic perspective has the following aims Bunge, 1998:436-437, Vol. 1):

1. To systematise knowledge.

2. To explain social facts.

3. To increase knowledge acquisition.

4. To test hypotheses and their relation to other hypotheses.

5. To guide research.

6. To provide a map for a complex terrain.

Working with theory leads to the researcher working in a qualitatively different way than if he/she is only concerned with data collection and relationships between the data collected.

Theory development does not necessarily presuppose a large amount of data. The scope of the data may prevent theories becoming irrelevant. In the same way as data collection without direction by theory can lead to irrelevant information, theory development without data can lead to knowledge of little use. It is not possible to say with certainty how much data must be available before starting theory development.

Regardless of how theories are constructed, it is important to be aware of the fact that they only say something about certain aspects of reality; no theory can cover all aspects of the reality we want to describe and explain (and to possibly predict future developments). Therefore, rival theories are necessary in order to achieve the greatest possible depth of explanation about a problem or phenomenon. Rival theories may be compared to two people taking a photo of an object *simultaneously* standing in different positions. In other words, their positions relative to the object will be at least slightly different, and in most cases very different, resulting in photos that show the object from different perspectives. In this manner, different aspects of the object are made available to an observer (Asplund, 1970). In a similar way, rival theories reveal different aspects and perspectives of a phenomenon or problem we want to illuminate. Thus, theories covering the same phenomenon:

1. Will only cover certain aspects of a problem or phenomenon.
2. Are partial.

3. Are based on subjective selections of certain aspects of a problem or phenomenon. This also applies to using quantitative methods and quantitative indicators.

4. Present only partial truths about a problem or phenomenon.

The above description, however, may limit the scope of theories but does not make them less true. We should just be aware that theories, no matter how they are developed, cannot describe the full and whole truth. Any theory is an idealisation of reality and will contain one or another form of simplification: in the selection of certain aspects of the problem or phenomenon, in the choice of problem question, research questions and methodology, and in how we choose to highlight the results (Asplund, 2010).

For researchers, theories should be a help to direct attention in the research process. Thus, the theory can provide guidance for selecting problem areas for empirical research (Merton, 1967:5).

How are theories developed? What are the elementary building blocks and how are these put together? When developing theories, should one start with data or begin with hypotheses?

The building blocks of a theory are always propositions in a systemic perspective. Propositions contain concepts. A concept that belongs to a theory can be called theoretical if it is:

1. Unique to the theory, or

2. Specifically clarifies the theory.

Propositions in a theory are either premises (postulates), definitions or consequences of terms. Once a system of postulates and definitions has been created and organised, an essential condition may have been fulfilled but this is not sufficient in theory development. To proceed we must expand the system with propositions that are related to each other (Bunge, 1983; 1983a).

There is considerable consensus among researchers that any actual theory should be based on data. However, there are still three reasons why data elements should not exist in the actual theory: The theory should be (1) general, (2) testable and (3) predictable.

A theory of social systems can be assessed from the practical value it has for a user of the theory. An example of such a theory is Asplund's "motivation theory"[84]. This mini-theory may be written as: **People are motivated by social response.** It can be applied in practical

[84] Asplund's "motivation theory" is constructed (framed) here by the authors of the chapter on the basis of two of Asplund's books (Asplund, 1970; 2010).

organizational contexts; for instance, by leaders who want to improve the performance of knowledge workers. Another example of a mini-theory that has practical relevance for leaders is North's "action theory"[85], which may be written as: **People act on the basis of a system of rewards as expressed in the norms, values, rules and attitudes in the culture (the institutional framework).** If we combine Asplund's motivation theory and North's action theory we arrive at the following practical theory: **People are motivated by the social responses that the institutional framework rewards.** This theory can be tested and applied by organizational studies in practical contexts.

Conclusions

Conclusion I: Answer to the problem question

The problem question that has been discussed in the chapter is: How can we develop a general scientific methodology, on tenets from Mario Bunges philosophy?

The answer to the problem question is that in the systemic perspective we clarify our assumptions, and emphasise a thorough analysis of the problem to be investigated. Then we develop a problem question with

[85] North's "action theory" is constructed (framed) here by the authors of the chapter on the basis of a number of North's books: 1990; 1993; 1994; 1996; 1997.

related research questions. The research questions are designed so that they are operationalized. In addition, the systemic perspective is concerned with dynamic hypotheses and the application of theory.

Conclusion II: Theoretical implications

The systemic perspective and a general scientific methodology helps the researcher to apply appropriate rules, like in a complex game. For instance, if you are unsure about the rules that apply in a game such as chess, then you are obviously doomed to make mistakes and may be put into an embarrassing position. A systemic perspective can help us to do the right thing when procedures are crucial to the end result. It can also help researchers by pointing out that the knowledge one has about a phenomenon/problem may be based on faulty procedures. The hypothesis is quite simple: The more knowledge you acquire about a phenomenon/problem, the more likely it is that new gaps in the knowledge will appear. It is a systemic perspective, inter alia, that may help empirical scientific studies make improvements and so continuously fill revealed gaps in knowledge. A systemic perspective can be helpful in the following manner:

The perspective may be helpful when we need to clarify the problem to be investigated (Bunge, 1979:253-292), and when the problem and problem question need to be conceptualised.

Conclusion III: Practical implications for the student and researcher

To develop a conceptual model on the basis of the problem and problem question, it may be appropriate to take as a starting point some social facts, or as Bunge says: "a type of social system." Bunge, 1999:11). Examples of social systems are teams, institutions, private or public organisations, and NGOs. Once this has been done, someone selects some properties of the social system that are considered to be important for the **problem** and **problem question**, and which relate to other important properties. These properties are then designated by using concepts. The concepts are then formulated into **research questions** in the scientific investigation. Further, an assumption (reasoned guess) is made concerning the **relationships between the concepts** (research questions). Once this is done we will have established a preliminary **conceptual model** of the problem, the problem question and research questions. In such a conceptual model the problem question will constitute the core of the model, as shown in Fig. 1. The next step is the development of **indicators** for the research questions (elements of the model), so that issues can be examined in a practical context. Some theorists, including Bunge, term research questions "operationalised hypotheses"(Bunge, 1999:11).

When data, information and knowledge are collected and analysed, the original model may need to be corrected because new knowledge and insights have emerged in the investigation. In such a case, the revision of the model will be described, say, in a separate chapter; in this chapter, the new model will be explained, the application of the findings that have been acquired, and possibly the theory or theories that have been relied on to explain the new relationships in the revised model. The investigation is then concluded by generalising the new model so that it includes several concepts, variables and indicators. In this way, those that research the same problem and problem question may use it as a guideline for further research.

Conclusion IV: Further research

Asplund's motivation theory and North's action theory, as mentioned above, are mini-theories that should be tested in practice to see if they have relevance for the problems related to for instance leadership issues. If the theories are able to predict how people are motivated and which incentives they value, then the two mini-theories could be of great use in practical leadership contexts.

References

Adriaenssen, D.J. & Johannessen, J-A. (2015). Conceptual

generalisation:

Methodological reflections in social science, A systemic viewpoint, Kybernetes, The international journal of cybernetics, systems and management sciences, 44, 4: 588-605.

Asplund, J. (1970). Om undran innfør samhället, Argos, Stockholm.

Asplund, J. (2010). Det sociala livets elementära former, Korpen, Stockholm

Bateson, G. (1972). Steps to a Ecology of Mind, Intex Books, London.

Becker, G.S. (1976). The Economic Approach to Human Behavior, University of Chivago Press, Chicago.

Bunge, M. (1967). Scientific Research, Vol. 3, in studies of the foundations methodology and philosophy of science, Springer Verlag, Berlin.

Bunge, M. (1977). Treatise on basic philosophy. Vol. 3. Ontology I: The furniture of the world. Dordrecht, Holland: D. Reidel.

Bunge, M. (1979). Treatise on Basic Philosophy, Volume 4, Ontology II: A World of Systems, Reidel, Boston.

Bunge, M. (1983). Exploring the World, Reidel, Dordrecht.

Bunge, M. (1983a). Understanding the World: Epistemology & Methodology II, Dordrecht: Reidel.

Bunge, M.   (1985). Philosophy of Science and Technology, Part I, Reidel, Dordrecht.

Bunge, M.   (1985a). Philosophy of Science and Technology, Part II, Reidel, Dordrecht.

Bunge, M. (1996). Finding philosophy in social science. New Haven: Yale University Press,

Bunge, M. (1997). Mechanism and explanation. Philosophy of the Social Sciences 27: 410- 465.

Bunge, M. (1998). Social Science under Debate: A Philosophical Perspective, University of Toronto Press, Toronto.

Bunge, M. (1998a). Philosophy of science: From explanation to justification, Volume two, Transaction Publishers, New Jersey.

Bunge, M. (1999). Dictionary of Philosophy, Prometheus Books, Amherst, New York.

Bunge, M. & Ardila, R. (2012). Philosophy of Psychology, Springer

Deleuze, G. & Guattari, F. (2011). What is Philosophy, Verso,

London.

Dubin, R. **(1969).** Theory Building, The Free Press, New York.

Durkheim, E. **(2013).** The Rules of Sociological Method, Palgrave, New York.

Feyerabend, P.K. **(1990).** Realism and the history of Knowledge, I W.R. Shea & A. Spadafora (ed.). Creativity in the Arts and Science, pp. 142-153, Science History Publications, Canton, MA.

Hernes, G. **(1998).** Real virtuality, in social mechanisms: An analytical approach to social theory, edited by Peter Hedstrøm and Richard Swedberg, Cambridge University Press, Cambridge (pp. 74-102).

Johannessen, J-A. (1996). Systemics Applied to the Study of Organizational Fields:Developing

Systemic Research Strategy for Organizational Fields". Kybernetes, vol. 25, 1: 33-51.

Johannessen, J-A. (1997). Aspects of causal processes, Kybernetes, Vol. 26, nr. 1: 30-52.

Johannessen, J-A. (1997a) Philosophical problems with the design and use of information systems, Kybernetes, 26, 3:30-48.

Johannessen, J-A. (1997b). Aspects of ethics in systemic thinking, Kybernetes, No.26, 9. 983-

1001

Johannessen, J-A. (1998). Organizations as social systems: the search for a systemic theory of organizational innovation processes, Kybernetes,27,4: 359-387.

Johannessen, J-A. & Olaisen, J. (2005) Systemic philosophy and the philosophy of social science – Part I: Transcendence of the naturalistic and the anti-naturalistic position in the philosophy of social science, Kybernetes, Vol. 34 Iss: 7/8, pp.1261 - 1277

Johannessen, J-A. & Olaisen, J. (2005a) Systemic philosophy and the philosophy of social science: Part II: the systemic position, Kybernetes, Vol. 34 Iss: 9/10, pp.1570 - 1586

Latour, B. & Woolgar, s. (1986). Laboratory Life: The Construction of Scientific Facts, Princeton University Press, Princeton.

Miller, J. G. (1978). Living Systems, McGill, New York.

North, D.C. (1990). Institutions, Institutional Change and economic performance, Cambrifge University Press, Cambridge.

North, D. (1993). Nobelforedraget:

http://www.nobelprize.org/nobel_prizes/economics/laureates/1993/no

rth-lecture.html#not2, lesedato, 4.5.2012.

North, D.C. (1994). Economic performance through time, American

Economic Review, 84: 359-368.

North, D.C. (1996). Epilogue: Economic performance through time. In

Alston, L.J.; Eggertson, T. & North, D.C. "Empirical studies in

institutional change", Cambridge University Press, Cambridge (pp.342-

355).

North, D.C. (1997). Prologue, 3-13 in J.N. Drobak & J.V.C. The

frontiers of the new institutional economics, Academic Press, New York.

Merton, R.K. (1967). Social Theory and Social Structure, Free Press,

London.

Miller, J.G. (1978). Living Systems, McGraw-Hill, New York.

Popper, K.R. (1976). The open society and its enemies, Routledge &

Kegan

Paul, London.

Turner, J.H. (1988). A Theory of Social Interaction, Polity Press, New York.

Turner, J.H. (1991). The Structure of Sociological Theory, Wadsworth Publishing Company, Belmont, California.

Index

113
Attribution, 15

B

Boudon-Coleman diagram, 37
boundaries, 65, 67
Bunge, 37, 43, 80

C

Case-Study, 25, 46
circular, 10, 54, 62, 63, 77, 91
communication, iv, 52, 53, 54, 55, 57,
58, 59, 60, 61, 63, 64, 68, 69, 71,
72, 73, 74, 75, 76, 77, 78, 102, 103
concepts, 5, 6, 7, 9, 10, 11, 15, 19, 20,
21, 29, 32, 53, 61, 110, 113, 114
conceptual, iii, 2, 3, 4, 5, 7, 8, 9, 10, 11,
12, 13, 15, 16, 18, 19, 20, 30, 31,
32, 33, 34, 36, 37, 39, 61, 77, 83,
90, 98, 113
conceptual generalisation, 2, 4, 5, 20,
34, 36
conceptual model, 4, 5, 8, 9, 10, 11, 18,
20, 30, 113
Condition, 70
construct, 21, 22, 91, 94, 102
context, 13, 17, 21, 25, 27, 28, 29, 30,
32, 33, 34, 63, 68, 74, 91, 97, 105,
114
creative destruction, 17
criteria, 36, 62, 89, 97, 103
cybernetics, 85, 116

D

Data mining, 12, 28
data mining models, 29
dead souls, 60
description, 60, 87, 99, 103, 109
distinction, iv, 52, 53, 54, 55, 58, 62,
64, 65, 66, 67, 70, 71, 72, 73, 74,
77, 78, 85

dynamic hypotheses, 101, 102, 103,
112

E

ecosystem, 54
emergence, 39, 44, 92
empirical, 2, 3, 7, 10, 11, 13, 15, 20,
21, 22, 23, 29, 32, 33, 70, 94, 98,
106, 109, 112
empirical generalisation, 2, 3
epistemology, 84
expectations, 56, 63, 65, 66, 67, 78,
106
experiments, 5, 12, 13, 14, 15, 18
explanations, 38, 95, 102, 103

F

feedback, 59, 60
feedback loops, 59
framework, 19, 20, 32, 68, 111
Functional differentiation, 75, 92

H

hypotheses, 14, 23, 25, 29, 86, 88, 101,
102, 103, 104, 106, 107, 110, 114
hypotheses testing, 25

I

implications, 4, 13, 33, 36, 37, 71, 73,
97, 112, 113
information, 7, 9, 17, 20, 24, 26, 28,
29, 34, 53, 56, 60, 62, 63, 76, 77,
89, 99, 102, 103, 108, 114, 119
innovation, 17, 20, 26, 27, 101, 119
interpretation, 53, 57, 58, 63, 64, 65,
66, 67, 73, 75, 77, 78

K

kausalitet, 72

ABOUT THE AUTHOR

Jon-Arild Johannessen holds a Msc. from Oslo University in History. He holds a Ph.D. from Stockholm University in

Systems thinking. He is currently professor (full) at **Kristiania University College**, Oslo and **Nord University**, Norway. He has been professor (full) at Syd-danske University, Denmark, The Arctic University, Norway, and Norwegian School of Management.